'If you believe the only thing funnier than a member of the opposition being run out without facing a ball is one of your own team suffering the same fate, then village cricket is for you ... Berkmann's average is pitifully low – double figures are but a distant landmark for him. But, then again, this is the norm in his team: *Zimmer Men* is a lament for non-existent rather than fading talent' Nick Greenslade, *Observer*

'Fellow [cricket] addicts will recognise themselves. Non-addicts will also laugh, because the book is both truthful and crazed' P. J. Kavanagh, *Spectator*

'Berkmann's skill as a writer is in inverse proportion to his ability at cricket ... He engages the reader continuously with a rat-tat-tat of pithy tales and amusing asides that ensures the book coasts along in a way that poor Berkmann never does when batting' Christian Wolmar, *Oldie*

'There's plenty of sad old gits who will buy it. I would' Peter Wilby, *New Statesman*

'During the course of the last decade, Berkmann has witnessed all manner of change to the game at its most junior level and he gives each amendment, trend and innovation the same wonderfully observant, immensely funny treatment ... *Zimmer Men* is as funny as *Rain Men*, the type of book that makes you periodically burst into laughter which, let's face it, is a much-needed commodity in any sport' *Birmingham Post*

'The funniest cricket book of the year. Marcus Berkmann's unmissable *Zimmer Men* charts the unsteady progress of his Sunday cricket team into middle age' Simon O'Hagan, *Independent*

Zimmer Men

THE TRIALS AND TRIBULATIONS OF THE AGEING CRICKETER

MARCUS BERKMANN

ABACUS

ABACUS

First published in Great Britain in 2005 by Little, Brown
This paperback edition published in 2006 by Abacus
Reprinted 2006

Some of the material in this book originally appeared in a different
form in *Wisden Cricket Monthly* (now *The Wisden Cricketer*,
www.thewisdencricketer.co.uk).

The publisher is grateful for permission to reproduce extracts from
Wisden's Cricketer's Almanack (2002 edition), courtesy of The Wisden
Group; and from *Third Man to Fatty's Leg* (2004) by Steve James,
courtesy of First Stone Publishing.

A CIP catalogue record for this book
is available from the British Library.

ISBN-13: 978-0-349-11915-1
ISBN-10: 0-349-11915-5

Papers used by Abacus are natural, recyclable products made from
wood grown in sustainable forests and certified in accordance with
the rules of the Forest Stewardship Council.

Typeset in Bembo by M Rules
Printed and bound in Great Britain by
Clays Ltd, St Ives plc
Paper supplied by Hellefoss AS, Norway

Abacus
An imprint of
Little, Brown Book Group
Brettenham House
Lancaster Place
London WC2E 7EN

A Member of the Hachette Livre Group of Companies

www.littlebrown.co.uk

CONTENTS

INTRODUCTION

It is a glorious sunny day in July. In north London, where I live, the air smells faintly of exhaust and sweat. A plague of genetically modified mosquitoes has recently been wafted over the Channel by a freak gust, and I have weals and welts on every limb. The shop up the road has run out of ice cream, and one of my windows seems to be rotting away and could easily fall on someone (such as me, should I happen to be walking under it at the time). What's more, I am skint and hungover and my hair has reached that stage in the growing cycle when it looks suspiciously like a wig. Life is far from sweet, but, even so, I am in a terrifically good mood. For today is Sunday, and we are playing our annual game against Charlton-on-Otmoor. And this year, I believe, we might have a chance of beating them.

This is a village we have been playing for many years. For a while we played them in May, and if their football team was having a good run in the cup, their cricket team would be denuded of all the talent. In those years we had a chance. Sometimes we took that chance. A couple of our bowlers have recorded their best figures there. Others have recorded their worst. For at full strength Charlton-on-Otmoor can be a handful. Their opening batsman Barry, who says very little, has two scores against us, 0 and lots. And they have always had a couple of those batters who come in at five and six, look as though they could get out any second, and suddenly take the game away from you, biff bash bosh. The bowlers, several generations of Coopers and Launchburys, don't mess about either. But the fixture endures. We like them, they seem to like us, and their teas are sublime. Indeed, the cakes and sandwiches very nearly make up for the pitch, upon which sheep must surely graze between matches. Either they creep in at night when no one is watching or they are bused in especially. Normally you would pray for a little rain before the Charlton-on-Otmoor game. Rain takes a bit of the sting out. During a hot spell you fear for your teeth, among other useful body parts. How the pitch plays today will depend to some extent on how much grass they have left, and, to a greater extent, on how much managed to grow in the first place.

It rained yesterday, rather heavily I'm told, which is good news. What you need at Charlton-on-Otmoor is what we don't usually have: lots of good bowlers. This week we thought we had them. We had two excellent openers: one steady and accurate, the other one slightly quicker than he looks, and he looks quite quick. At first change we had one of our most reliable bowlers, in that he loves bowling long spells in which he gives nothing away. Usually we would have to open the bowling with him; this week we would be able to save him up, stick him on at one end and unleash our spinners at the other. Unleash? Am I really using that word? Our two best spinners, who both give the ball the most fearful tweak, are as mercurial and unpredictable as many of their species: one day lethal, the next day rubbish. But both have been taking hatfuls of wickets. Their confidence is high, and that's what matters in this game. This absurd, enthralling, unforgiving game.

Yesterday came the phone call. It was the quick bowler. He had just wrenched his back carrying the shopping. He was lying down on the floor and he couldn't move. He was terribly sorry but . . . I got him off the phone as quickly as I could. There was a possible replacement, a batsman not a bowler, who was desperate to play. I rang him. Astoundingly he was still free and happy to play. This was a good omen. We may not have our strike bowler, but we still have eleven men and we are not bad.

All that stands between us and possible victory today is Phil, the Charlton captain. Phil is a big bloke. He has a robust sense of humour. He bowls quickly and hits the ball with Flintoff-like power. He has been playing for the village for three years now, and we have yet to get him out. Last year he scored a century and hit successive overs for 21 and 22 runs. It was the single at the end of the first over to farm the strike that I admired the most. He is the backbone of Charlton's team and quite a lot of the other bones as well. If he is unwell today, or injured, or has been arrested on trumped-up murder charges in a shocking miscarriage of justice, we could yet prevail.

At 11.23 a.m. Terence drops by to give me a lift to the game. We blither and drivel all the way up the M40. I am happy because I am looking forward to the game. Terence is happy because he is driving his new convertible. Press one button and the roof retracts automatically in a series of ergonomically complicated manoeuvres that are explicitly designed to impress men like me and Terence. We arrive at the pub in high spirits, and following ancient tradition Terence buys me a drink to avoid having to buy a larger round when other people turn up.

We order lunch, and our team-mates filter in. As my roast beef arrives, Sam, one of our newest players, bursts through the door. Our other opening bowler, Andrew-with-the-ponytail, has texted him to say that he has been out 'working' all night and is therefore too tired to play. This text was sent at 11.54 a.m.

Everyone is distraught. Several yorkshire puddings spontaneously collapse on their plates. Andrew's name and ponytail are now mud. He has shown signs of flakiness in the past, but nothing like this. Sam, who knows him well, assures us that he has been working, as opposed to 'working'. But what difference does it make? An hour before the game starts we have ten men and no opening bowlers.

As John Cleese says in the film *Clockwise*, 'It's not the despair. I can stand the despair. It's the hope.'

We turn up at the ground. Familiar faces, one year older than last time, say hello. One of them, I swear, is looking at my hair and wondering if it's a wig. Then out of the pavilion's double doors, bending his head down and pulling in his shoulders to squeeze through, comes Phil. Huge smile. Proffers hand. I shake it, although it's about three times the size of mine. We walk out to the wicket. It looks all right, although I have been playing long enough to know that I know absolutely nothing about pitches. 'It should play pretty well,' says Phil, prodding it lovingly and eyeing the short straight boundaries. The cows in the next field have a strange reddish tinge, from all the lost balls they have eaten.

Phil wins the toss. Barry and a young lad walk out to open the batting. Barry is concentrating hard. We have been playing here for so many years that promising tearaway opening batsman Barry has become weathered, stalwart, pillar-of-the-community Barry, and he still scores loads of runs. The young lad quickly runs himself out and Phil walks to the wicket. I gulp.

Let's cut straight to the punchline. There's no need for you to suffer as well.

In forty-one overs Charlton-on-Otmoor compile 329 for the loss of that one wicket. Barry scores 172 not out, Phil 124 not out. Not for a moment does either consider retiring. Most of us do, though. Running off, leaping into our cars and never playing this stupid bloody game again. It is carnage. None of our bowlers comes close to taking a wicket. Several balls are lost. Numbers four and five in the Charlton batting order sit seething throughout. The wicket, which seems to be saturated, never does a thing, but even so, we feel we do quite well to score 91. Phil, I should add, sportingly brings himself on as seventh bowler and takes two for 4 in ten balls. We lose by 238 runs. That's not bad for an afternoon.

And there's only a week to go until the next game.

1

OLD

Like village cricket, middle age is a cruel business. It creeps up on you when you are not looking, like a bloke with a cosh. Even though you know it's coming, and you keep looking behind you just in case, it arrives so much earlier and more swiftly than you had expected that it still takes you completely by surprise. As children would say, it's not fair. Childhood, after all, takes decades. To a six-year-old, even a shortish car journey takes several weeks. Youth drags on interminably, like a 78 r.p.m. record slowed down to 33. And then, finally, the glory years of the thirties arrive. For many of us this is the first time in our lives when we look OK, if we say so ourselves. And we feel OK, too: confident and comfortable, and able to deal with the world on even terms, with shoulders back and chin jutting out. (Don't try this at home: you may fall over.) This golden era, in reality, lasts less than a Durham first innings. Before you have had time to take advantage, it's gone, and you are suddenly past it, a wheezing old wreck, invisible to women once again. As an Australian friend put it to me recently, it's a pisser.

The vicious, squealing irony in all this is that, in your head, you're brighter and funnier and cleverer than you ever were, and possibly slightly more mature as well. It's only your body that is letting you down. Years ago, back in the 1970s, during tea intervals in Tests, I remember a little pro-gramme on ITV called *Looks Familiar,* hosted by Denis Norden, who at that time can only have been in his forties. It was a nostalgia quiz – the very first of its type, in fact, and I'm sure there are people who would say now that nostalgia quizzes aren't what they used to be. At the beginning of each show Denis would chucklingly attempt to define middle age, mainly in terms of snoek and Gracie Fields and other long-forgotten cornerstones of popular culture. Mad that I should be watching such rubbish, although the alternative on BBC1 was Peter West filling in time chatting with Tom Graveney on the roof of the pavilion, and the two of them desperately trying to think of something interesting to say while 80 m.p.h. winds blew the cameraman over the edge to his death.

When you reach middle age yourself, though, you find that it has a very simple definition. Middle age is when you look in the mirror and realise that you look and feel as good as you will ever look and feel. That's not to say that you are at some sort of peak; it's just that from here on in, things are only going to get worse. You can try and resist the march of time, but you do so at boundless risk to your own dignity. Wigs, corsets and Paul McCartney-style mahogany hair colourings were invented to make ageing people look even older, especially when placed next to Paul McCartney-style younger wives. Not that many of us in the cricket team are quite at that stage. But we will be sooner or later. A few of us have bought midlife-crisis convertibles to give us something nicer to think about.

Sport can help. Well, some sports can. Not many of our number still play football, and those who do must suffer a string of painful and avoidable injuries, as their ageing legs are sliced beneath them by psychotic younger opponents. There's golf, I suppose. (Does that count as a sport?) I went to a friend's golf-club quiz night recently. He wanted to win because he is naturally competitive. But he also wanted not to win because he didn't want to 'make a bad impression' on the tiny-brained snobs and dullards who controlled the club. You could see the pinched expressions of disapproval all around as, almost in tears, my friend went up to accept third prize. So, not golf then.

I would have suggested marathon running had another friend not strained and wrenched virtually every muscle in his body training for the London Marathon. He still calls himself a runner, but I can't remember when he was last fit enough to put on a pair of shorts without flinching. No, it has to be cricket, as always. Cricket has nurtured our souls for years. We know where we are with it. We are the sort of people who switch on the TV to look up page 341 on

Ceefax, then watch the programmes as an afterthought. We are the people who still blub when they watch their now worn and irreplaceable tapes of Botham's Ashes. We practise our cover drives in the mirror with serving spoons and garden implements. We have fond memories of Chris Tavaré. We cannot encounter the number 111 in normal daily life without thinking of David Shepherd hopping.

I first fell under cricket's spell in the historic summer of 1971, when Pakistan and India were the visiting Test teams. I vaguely remember Zaheer Abbas scoring one of his vast double centuries earlier in the summer, although – being eleven and extremely well behaved – I may well have been at school at the time. But it was the dibbly-dobbly medium-pace bowling of Abid Ali and Solkar that made the more lasting impression on me. I understood, because the commentators had told me, that these two were barely worthy of the description 'bowlers'. That their job was to come on and deliver a few harmless overs with the new ball to get rid of the shine and set things up for India's fearsome three-pronged spin attack. And yet, at Old Trafford, Abid Ali rattled through England's top order – Jameson, Edrich, Fletcher and D'Oliveira – to collect four for 64 and give India a faint aroma of victory (until Illingworth and Lever put on 168 for the eighth wicket and restored normality). I was mesmerised by this. On some level I think I began to understand the essence of all sport: that none of it makes any sense and that anyone who thinks they know for certain what will happen is a fool. Or maybe I just liked the clothes.

I don't know: it was a long time ago. But from that day on I was hooked.

It helped, of course, that in those days England were pretty good. Before the India series they had been unbeaten in twenty-five Tests. A year later they retained the Ashes and drew 2–2 with a terrifying-looking Australian team (Stackpole, two Chappells, K.D. Walters, Marsh, Lillee and Massie). This series also introduced me to the commentary of Richie Benaud, who in those days used to come over only for the Australian Tests. In 1973 there occurred one of those pivotal moments in a lifetime that change everything. We were on holiday in the Mediterranean somewhere, sitting at a bar. My brother and I, nine and thirteen respectively, were bored out of our minds. And then I saw, on the back page of someone's *Daily Express* at a neighbouring table, that Frank Hayes of Lancashire, on his Test debut, had scored 106 not out in the second innings. A terrible pang hit me. I had not seen this innings on TV. I didn't know what anybody else had scored or even what the result was. And I'd never heard of Frank Hayes of Lancashire. I asked my father for the money to buy a *Daily Express*. He told me to piss off. This, then, was my first cricketing bereavement. I mourned for the Test match I hadn't witnessed personally. Fancy missing the flowering of an exciting new talent. After we got back, of course, Hayes barely scored another run. I wasn't so egomaniacal to believe that this was my fault. That came later, when like everyone else I developed one of those psychopathologies that convinces you that, if you leave the room for a moment to put the kettle on, England will lose a wicket. But it did kickstart a series of dreams that continue to this day: that I am on holiday somewhere, and that England are playing a Test match with all sorts of players I haven't heard of, and all I can see of it is the odd snatched headline on someone else's newspaper and I'm screaming and then I wake up. This is the true madness of cricket.

There had to be a solution to all this, so at university I and some friends formed a cricket team, which we named the Captain Scott Invitation XI. We were inspired by the legendary polar explorer, who, though resolutely stiff of upper lip, had a fairly poor record in his core activity of polar exploring. Roald Amundsen, who beat him to the South Pole, had taken huskies, as recommended in all the books. Scott eschewed these hardy little dogs and took horses, which all died, as did he and his men on the way back home. 'For God's sake look after our people,' he wrote on his deathbed, little realising that sixty-five years later some larky students would despoil his reputation in pursuit of their own brand of cricketing mediocrity.

The problem was that most of us who wanted to play had not played much cricket before. I had been to a minor public school in north London where sporting ability was valued far higher than academic excellence, or indeed anything other than large charitable bequests from sentimental old boys. If you had no obvious talent for cricket – and I hadn't – then they never let you within a field's length of a cricket bat, and sent you off instead to do cross-country runs across the evil child-eating bogs of Hampstead Heath. Some of the finest people I have known lost their lives in those quagmires. I and my friend Harry only got into Oxford because our headmaster had told us to our faces that we had no chance, and we were determined to prove him wrong. When we turned up in October 1978, the first thing we noticed was the glorious profusion of slightly underused cricket pitches. Forming our own cricket team wasn't just an option; it felt more like an obligation.

You start out young and naive and fresh-faced, and slightly spotty to be honest, and a bit gawky, and maybe even nerdy, and only just aware that it's uncool to quote *Monty Python*'s dead-parrot sketch in any circumstances that find you awake. A quarter of a century later you are still playing cricket with some of the same people, amazingly, but the intervening years have left their mark. Heads that once boasted luxuriant growths of hair are now wholly reflective, and occasionally used to blind incoming batsmen. Stomachs have grown in most directions. Legs, though they move just as fast when they run, don't seem to cover anywhere near as much ground. Everyone has kids or a midlife-crisis convertible. Some players have given up, and one or two have vanished from our lives for ever. New players have replaced them. We are all ageing together, which at least means we have company.

What hasn't changed is that one day every weekend during the summer we set off in our cars at about 11.23 in the morning to meet at a distant pub, drink more beer than we should (and less than we would like to) and then play cricket in scenic surroundings against teams who are usually better than we are. I marvel that we have managed to get away with it for so long. Not that we ever acknowledge this to each other, for to mention it at all would be to risk breaking the spell. So we pretend that it's something rather routine that we just happen to do, for we are blokes and that is how we behave. And yet, as the years dribble by, we become more and more aware of the fragility of the whole thing. Many of us are in our forties now. We know we don't have much cricketing time left. Twenty-five years, maybe – thirty at the absolute limit. Time enough to score that elusive century, or take that elusive wicket. We hope.

My previous book about village cricket, *Rain Men,* was written when we were all in our mid-thirties, hopelessly unaware that the glory years were soon to come to an end. This book takes the story on another ten years, into the unexplored territory of middle age, and maybe even beyond. (Its working title was *Last of the Summer Wides.)* It asks whether it is entirely dignified for men of our age to go on playing cricket, and then feigns deafness to avoid hearing the answer. It sneers at young people, their useless music, their bad hairstyles and their bullet-like throws from the long boundary. It looks back in anger, and looks forward in terror. And on Amazon it spots a new remastered DVD of Botham's Ashes, and buys it with a single click.

2

SCOTTS

Four of us started the Captain Scott Invitation XI at university, and when we left we took it with us. Terence, Richard and I had met on our first day there, and they are still two of my closest friends. Terence had never played cricket before Scotts, and after decades behind the stumps still sometimes gives the same impression. For some years he has laboured under the nickname The Human Sieve. But Terence was and is no fool. By agreeing always to go number eleven when he keeps wicket, he has made the wicketkeeping position his own. Every captain needs a player like Terence: a willing number eleven who, furthermore, usually gives him a lift to the match.

Richard was the only one of us who had played much cricket before, so we made him captain. This turned out to be a mistake, for Richard was too governed by crazed whims to make an effective leader. Uninterested in tactics, he would open the bowling with a purveyor of donkey-drops just to see what happened, and would never put any fielders behind square on the leg side because he didn't think bowlers should bowl there. His period as captain was characterised by defeat. All he was trying to do, in his slightly indirect way, was tell us that he didn't want to be captain. After one or two even less successful experiments, Harry and I took on the captaincy ourselves. Harry would captain on Saturdays and I would captain on Sundays, for by our fifth or sixth season we usually had two fixtures a weekend. Harry was also our fixtures secretary, and a remarkably diligent and assiduous one at that. Every weekend in the summer had as many games as it could hold. Bank holiday weekends commonly had three. Only weekends that happened to coincide with Harry's holidays abroad were mysteriously free of fixtures. Pure coincidence, he would say. No one wanted to play us on those weekends. We would look at him askance but let him get away with it, as none of us wanted to do the fixtures. Every team in the world needs a Harry. Ours just happened to be the Harriest.

I have known him now for nearly thirty-five years, since we were nine years old in Mr Walton's class, 2A. In that time we have worked together – he is a writer too, and a highly successful TV producer – bickered non-stop, stolen girl-friends from each other and generally behaved as disgracefully towards each other as you do to your oldest friend. We ran Captain Scott together for many years, but, as time went on, the two of us realised we had different ideas about what we wanted the team to be. Scotts had started out as a team of oddballs, many of whom had never played cricket before. As it developed we gained new oddballs who had played cricket before, but maybe hadn't found the team to suit their talents. Indeed, one or two of these oddballs had actually been thrown out of several teams who had failed to appreciate what they had to offer. I think immediately of Arvind, the diminutive solicitor from Delhi, who always fielded like a terrier to his own bowling, and like a fat, asthmatic terrier which had had all its legs amputated to everyone else's. Some of these oddballs you grew to like; others, like Arvind, you grew to dislike slightly less. We kept him, and one or two others, because they were good, and we needed some good players to counterbalance the likes of Terence and me.

I was, and remain, a negligible cricketer. A little bit of coaching, and years of ruler practice in the front room, have given me a serviceable forward defensive, but sadly little else. My speciality is the dogged 3 not out, low in the order, saving a match or, more usually, trying to save a match while watching everybody else get out at the other end. Occasionally I take a catch, which I'll make look harder than it is. I never bowl, for like all non-bowlers I live in fear of the never-ending over, in which wide follows wide follows wide until the earth cracks open under your feet and swallows you in shame.

So, as you can imagine, I am quite well disposed towards the concept of a mixed-ability side. If Captain Scott had not been mixed-ability I would never have got a game, let alone been captain for twenty years. Harry too started out as an out-and-out rabbit with the bat, also bowling a tidy if unthreatening medium pace. But Harry is a remarkably dedicated and single-minded individual. In another life he would have made an excellent medieval warlord. In the way that people are supposed to, he worked hard at his game, and turned himself into an obdurate opening batsman and a rather useful bowler, nagging and rhythmic with a good high action. Harry also discovered that he liked to win. Good grief, yes. He liked the team to win and he liked to play as large a part in that win as possible. If that meant him staying in for thirty-five overs to score an agonising 42 not out, then that was what it took. And if no one else got a bat or a bowl, that too was a price worth paying. Even though, as everyone else constantly pointed out, it wasn't ever he who paid the price.

And so the tenor of the team began to change. The less adept players found themselves marginalised when Harry was captaining, and some of them stopped playing when Harry was captaining, which suited him fine. I didn't mind either, as I was much happier running a team full of old lags, who after all were my friends. The Saturday and Sunday teams became quite distinct. Saturday teams tended to be young, fit and rather good. Sunday teams were older, chubbier and increasingly useless. Harry played both games every weekend because he played every game. Indeed, he had never missed a game. Last time I asked, the Captain Scott Invitation XI had played around 650 games, and Harry had played them all.

Years ago we all felt a bit threatened by this monomania, and tried surprisingly hard to sabotage his record (without much success, obviously). But these feelings passed. After a decade or two we even became quite proud of him. No other team we encountered had anyone as mad as this. Harry had been injured more times than I could mention, and had been unable to bowl for whole seasons. But the obsession went deep, into depths most people may not even have. Whatever the circumstances, whatever the weather, Harry would be on the field at the start of a game tossing the coin with the opposing captain, and then putting the other team in to give him the option of batting out time for a draw later in the day. Everything would be as it should be.

When I wrote *Rain Men* in 1994–5, the situation seemed to have stabilised. We effectively had two different teams, a Saturday team and a Sunday team, who didn't much like each other. But I didn't worry, as most cricket teams don't like each other. This, I decided, was the essential truth of village cricket: that in friendly games, without anything terribly important to fight for, most teams turned inwards. Even in league teams, where possible promotion to Division 8 dominates all conscious thought, everybody was slagging off everybody else. To their face or behind their back? It didn't matter. (Why choose? Why not both?) For cricket, as we all know, is not a team game, but a game for highly motivated individuals who pretend it's a team game. We had quite a few highly motivated individuals in our team – on a good day, somewhere approaching eleven.

Very slowly, though, it was dawning on me that in my unacknowledged battle with Harry for the heart and soul of the team, I was losing. True, I was the signatory on the cheque book, and I still captained most of the Sunday games, but my old friends were playing fewer and fewer games. They had all hit their mid-thirties. Many were married with children. They couldn't play cricket every weekend any more, even if they wanted to, and most didn't. But Harry was still arranging two games a weekend throughout the summer. The new regulars were the younger players who had the time to commit to all this. The old regulars felt disenfranchised. They would come along to a game every few weeks and barely recognise anyone. They said it wasn't fun any more.

In village cricket people don't really move teams. Some years ago I met a player who, after a series of business disasters, had moved to a smaller house three villages away. Fair enough, agreed his old team-mates, who understood the economic pressures of rural life as well as anyone. This player happily continued to play for his old team for several years. Then one day, filling in at the last moment, doing someone a favour, he played a game for his new village. His old team-mates were aghast. Apparently there had been some sort of row between the two teams some time in the 1950s, which had never been resolved. No one could remember what it was about, as everyone concerned was now dead. Nonetheless, this was a betrayal his old team could not countenance. They never selected him again.

Once you find your niche, you keep it, even if someone else wants it. Some teams regard enthusiastic newcomers almost as a threat. One bloke I know moved to a village (a different village) fifteen years ago and is still waiting for an extended run in the team. His son, having grown up there, is more likely to be accepted within the club, but even he can forget about becoming captain or wicketkeeper. These, it transpires, are hereditary posts.

Touring sides do not have the luxury of such rigidity. In Scott we always had to be on the lookout for new players to replace those who had stomped off in a huff after one atrocious lbw decision too many. Touring teams always need new blood; without it, they die. But even with all the changes I always felt we had a strong sense of team identity. No other side could lose so many balls in a single net session, or stonedrift so purposefully away from their allotted field positions.* This was where I belonged.

And then one day you don't. The realisation comes in a moment, although the process leading up to it may take several years. One day you just think, No, this isn't fun any more. I'd rather be doing something else. Crucially, I started

---

*Stonedrifting is the practice of moving from your allotted place in the field to somewhere you are not needed at all. It is named after an early Captain Scott stalwart, Paul Stone, who could drift forty or fifty yards between balls without realising that he had moved a single foot. Some fielders stonedrift with astounding skill and timing, often disappearing from where they are supposed to be only seconds before a batsman offers an easy catch there.

to feel relieved when games were rained off. This was traumatic. You begin to doubt your faith in cricket itself. Has the game lost its hold, after all this time? Do you no longer care whether England lose by an innings, or just ten wickets?

But it's not cricket you have lost faith in, it's your cricket team. The spirit of the side had changed. My friends were drifting away. The new players liked Harry's way more than they liked mine. In 1997, my last season, I had played only eight of twenty-one completed games, batted five times, with four not-outs, scored 2 runs, at an average of 2.00. I had lost all interest and confidence and was seriously contemplating retirement.

Oh yes, the R word. The most frightening ten letters in the cricketing lexicon. Bear in mind that I was thirty-seven at the time. In top-level sport this makes you a relic of the Palaeozoic era. I still remember with a jolt when the footballer Peter Reid was picked for England at the age of thirty-four, and one of the tabloids described him as 'timelord Peter Reid'. But in village cricket you are in the prime of life at thirty-seven. Only in your late fifties do you approach veteran status, and aggressive sixty-five-year-old silly mid-offs are not unknown. (I heard recently of an eighty-eight-year-old wicketkeeper who is still playing, although not without consequences: apparently he has to be left in that crouching position all week in order to be ready for the big game on Saturday.)

So retirement would be premature. A more sensible

solution came from our sharp-toothed stockbroker Francis. Why not break away and start another team? Well, why not, I thought. Captain Scott had changed, and there was no way of changing it back. Time to move on. So a few days later I gathered together a group of fellow seniors in the bar owned and run by Cliff, our mercurial leg-spinner and run-out expert, and over copious beers we decided, rather to our amazement, to leave Captain Scott and start up on our own. If we aimed a little lower, playing fewer games at a slightly less competitive level, we might just start to enjoy it again. Admittedly, we would never see Harry score 42 not out off thirty-five overs ever again, but we felt we could handle that . . .

To this day Rain Men players regale each other with Harry stories when slightly drunk and full of good cheer. Like many other people who habitually teeter on the verge of outright barminess, he cannot understand why people talk about him, which of course helps him to behave with that absolute lack of self-consciousness that gets you talked about. Some people said I went a bit easy on Harry in the first book, but you have to remember that we were running a cricket team together at the time, and it doesn't pay to alien-ate your oldest friend to whom you talk on the phone a dozen times a week. I don't intend to now, either. He could easily have thrown an MCG-sized wobbler when I told him I was leaving to start another team, but he didn't, and he even broke into a smile when I told him the names of one or two of the players I was taking with me. The Captain Scott Invitation XI has continued to thrive without us, and his players, a much more loyal bunch than we ever were, regard him with great fondness. I suspect he may even have mellowed over the years, although I am sure he would dispute that with vigour.

The only problem is that many Harry stories involve an element of conflict, of people losing tempers, of bats being thrown and of cars being driven away in high dudgeon. There was, notoriously, the game at Tusmore Park in which Harry batted for several days and eventually notched up a fifty; it may even have been his first. But his long and agonising vigil at the crease had driven the rump of non-batting spectators to the brink of revolt. When he eventually returned to the pavilion there was a notable lack of applause. I was out in the middle umpiring at the time, but even I could sense the *froideur*. Francis the sharp-toothed stockbroker and my old friend Richard were particularly incensed, and gave him the most arctic of shoulders. Harry went ballistic. His view was that they should be grateful for his long innings, and not resentful for missing the opportunity to play one themselves. You could see his point, but they didn't want to, and he couldn't see theirs. There's something wonderfully reassuring, when umpiring in the balmy and peaceful grounds of an imposing country house, to hear your team-mates back at the pavilion screaming at each other like Italians.

Other Harry stories tend to feature:

- Umpire giving Harry out lbw when he's on the front foot batting two feet outside his crease.
- Harry refusing to walk/walking only reluctantly.
- Insults exchanged between batsman and umpire/bats thrown across the field/refusal of other team to play us the following season.

What has never been in contention is his absolute single-mindedness. Self-doubt is a stranger to him. I remember an awkward incident at Charlton-on-Otmoor when Harry took a catch at long-off, right on the boundary. Neal was fielding twenty feet away, and thought he saw his foot go over the line. I was at deep mid-on and I thought I saw his foot go over the line. But Harry believed then (and believes to this day) that his foot did not go over the line, and because of his insistence the batsman was given out. I am not suggesting he cheated; in fact I don't believe he did. But years later whenever we go to Charlton, someone always recalls the incident; in both teams it has acquired the status of minor legend. This was in a game fifteen to twenty years ago, about which no one can remember anything else, let alone the result. For some reason it sticks in the mind. For some reason quite a lot of them stick in the mind.

3

MR FIXIT

What to call the new team? A number of possible names were bandied about. But after discounting the obscene, the dull, the overly whimsical and the aggressively meaningless, we found we had a short-list of none. I think it was Terence who came up with the idea of naming the team after my book *Rain Men*. Needless to say I cavilled and blustered, but eleven seconds later it was unanimously agreed that this was our best hope of getting new fixtures. It was 1 March, after all, and we had to be quick about it. Several years later I am writing a book about a cricket team named after a book written about another cricket team, but if that doesn't make you want to vomit, let's move on.

For the first time in my life I found myself having to put together a fixture list. Harry had always done this job for Scotts, and the rest of us had been delighted to let him get on with it. Now, the rest of them were delighted to let me get on with it. I was a little apprehensive, to say the least.

Until you have a game fixed up, you are not a cricket team. With one game, you are a cricket team for that day only. With two games you can start thinking of yourself as an occasional cricket team. With three or four you can start talking in public about 'our new team', although no one takes you quite seriously. Only with five can you start to plan the artefact that will validate your new team in the eyes of God and your possibly less-than-grateful wives and girl-friends: a fixture list.

It made for an anxious few weeks. By 1 March, I hadn't realised, virtually everyone has their fixture lists not only finished but wrapped up in ribbon and shiny paper. Some fixtures secretaries, especially those with scenic home grounds to play on (and therefore a queue of teams who want to come and play on them), have had the whole thing sorted out before Christmas. Others did it all immediately after Christmas, while a few, a precious few, left it all as late as possible and panicked some time in March. Harry had given me a couple of phone numbers of Oxfordshire teams Scotts had been playing for years. The likes of Charlton-on-Otmoor, Ardley-with-Fewcott and Tusmore Park, with whom we had always got on very well, would surely be well disposed towards our modest venture. As it was, two of them found space for us in their crowded schedules, and the third indicated a desire to play us the following year. We were up and running.

I had expected to arrange no more than six games in our first season, and with nothing done before 1 March would have been happy with four. But village cricket is like any social network: word gets around. Someone knows someone who knows someone else who runs a side you'd really get on with, and he knows someone who knows this wonderful pitch you can hire for not too much, and so on. One of our players arranged a fixture against his neighbours in Tooting. Another, who had moved out to Oxfordshire a couple of years before, brought in two fixtures and a glorious pitch on which to play them. In the end you don't feel that you have compiled a fixture list, so much as watched it spontaneously come into being. Games emerge, rather like popes. What seemed like a random drunken conversation at a party – because that's what it was – could and did turn, months later, into a phone call confirming a new game. Some fixtures breed new ones. Over the years, one or two Scott games have been so fertile they ended up presiding over huge extended fixture families. Other fixtures exist in solitude, curious one-offs in the list which occasionally become the most heated of grudge matches. Every new fixture is, in essence, a blind date. You'll play them, a little guardedly, and on your very best behaviour, trying not to shout too much and hoping that Tim the incredibly angry fast bowler doesn't shout 'You fucker!' when an umpire turns down his appeal. And if they like you enough, and you like them enough, and you both play the *right* sort of cricket (however you choose to define that), then you may agree to fix up a game the following year. This is by way of a second date. It's a fairly courtly start to a relationship, not unlike something out of Jane Austen.

'Miss Bennett, I suggest that we agree to start the game at 2.30 and that it shall be your responsibility on that occasion to provide the new ball.'

'Mr Darcy, that seems to me the most equitable arrangement.'

Even so, cricket fixtures may be the only blind dates to be called off because of persistent drizzle. Sometimes we have not played the other team, or even met them, until the third year of the fixture. Even Jane Austen would find that slow going.

For 1998 we ended up with nine fixtures, which felt like wealth beyond imagining. But because I had started arranging them so late, the first wasn't until mid-June. Never before had any of us had to wait so long for the first game of the season. The Scotts had been playing as usual since late April, and apparently sweeping all before them, as their new core of international athletes and South African *Übermenschen* asserted their authority over wheezing, elderly village sides. I had been intending to play for them once or twice, for old times' sake, but to my astonishment, after 285 games in nineteen years, I hadn't the remotest inclination to. I was unusual: in that first season a lot of players kept feet in both camps. Only Francis, who had grown tired of Scotts before any of us, declared his intention of playing only for Rain Men – although he would also be playing against us, for it was he who had set up a game against his neighbours in

Tooting, London SW19, and he had sensibly appointed himself their captain. This was our second fixture, and we would be playing it in the leafy idyll of Pembroke College, Oxford – a ground so stunningly beautiful that our various games there over the years had almost all been called off. (The ones on council pitches with syringes on a full length and squishy lakes of dogshit at deep mid-wicket, we always play to the last scheduled ball.)

Our first fixture was against an outfit calling themselves the Marquis of Hereford's XI. As always with a team name like that, you don't know whether it's the name of a pub or whether there really will be some seedy old gentleman watching the nice young men in their whites, before ambling back to his ancestral home (or sad shed). But we were all looking forward to the game with an excitement that verged on drooling madness. At least the weather should be OK. One reason for starting in June, I kept telling everyone, was that summer had usually started by then, neglecting to add that in some years it had finished by then as well. In a diary for *Wisden Cricket Monthly* I wrote:

By the time you read this we hope to have played our first game in the colours of our new team, Rain Men CC. I say 'we hope' because only a fool would make any further assumptions at this stage. British cricket may have built up a reputation for being a bit soft, but British weather takes no prisoners. If Alec Stewart's side could play with even half the aggression and purpose of our thundery showers, they would be unbeatable.

(Alec Stewart. Remember him?)

This was tempting fate. Indeed, so riled were the weather gods by my presumption that they redirected a large grey storm-cloud from the soggy wastes of the North Sea straight to the Marquis of Hereford XI's home ground in Cambridge. Our first fixture as Rain Men CC was rained off. How ironic. Ha ha ha.

Our second game had been arranged for the following Sunday. Suddenly there was a great deal at stake. There were no more games for three weeks. So if this one disappeared from the schedule, our inaugural season would not begin until the last week of July. 'England could have lost the Test series by then,' said Howard, our best batsman, who can hit an on-drive at will. We were all desperate to get going, partly to show the world we could do it, and partly because some of us hadn't played cricket all season, and could barely remember what you did with that long piece of wood with the rubber handle and the small leather sphere with the gold writing on each side. 'Don't worry about it,' said Howard. 'It doesn't matter. Lack of form is temporary, but lack of class is permanent.'

So you can imagine how close I was to mental breakdown on the Thursday before the Sunday, when I had just seven players booked in. The weather forecast promised unbroken hours of magnificent sunshine tempered by a subtle breeze through backward point. And yet I was seriously having to contemplate cancelling our first fixture because I couldn't raise a side.

It was, and wasn't, my fault. Having used up so much emotional energy arranging the game the previous weekend, I hadn't worked anywhere near as hard at recruiting a team for game two. Perhaps I had assumed that, overwhelmed by enthusiasm after our first magnificent defeat, players would just sign up willy-nilly for the rest of their natural lives.

But there was also the vexed problem of location. Francis had booked the wondrous Pembroke College pitch, but without first telling his team-mates. When they found out, they rebelled. They all lived in the same street in Tooting, SW19. They didn't want to go all the way to Oxford to play cricket. They didn't really want to go any further than Tooting, SW19. As someone who has frequently driven 100 miles to be told that the game had been cancelled on Tuesday, and didn't anyone tell us, I thought this was a bit soft, but it also appeared to be non-negotiable. I accepted the *fait accompli,* and Francis found an alternative venue a post-code away in Wandsworth, SW17.

Now it was my players' turn to rebel. Feeble excuses rolled in. We're moving house. It's Father's Day. Giant man-eating lizards have taken over at my employers and I'm having to work through the weekend. All they were saying, of course, was that they were perfectly happy to play at Pembroke, but were too soft for any pitch that might veer towards the municipal.

So on Thursday I had seven. Thankfully those seven rallied around. Someone's wife's cousin's boyfriend was signed up. Friends of friends were found, and didn't run away quickly enough. A small but enthusiastic child was placed on emergency standby. Somehow we crept up to eleven. Among them were two people who had never played cricket before, and two who had not played for twenty-five years.

I would be lying if I said we won. In truth, ignominious defeat was a foregone conclusion. But my, did we enjoy ourselves. The ground wasn't at all bad and the weather was kind. One of the two who had never played took a heroic catch in the deep. I scored 3, and thought I was going to die of exhaustion and heatstroke before I was bowled swiping pathetically. What had I forgotten to do while frantically sorting out games and filling teams? Only any exercise whatsoever. Best of all, though, was that Terence the Human Sieve, who customarily bats at number eleven, opened the batting and hit a swashbuckling 30, his highest-ever score. He would never have been able to do that playing for Scotts – at least, not any more. And we had all had a marvellous time. I couldn't remember enjoying a game of cricket so much. Then someone pointed out that we had three weeks to wait until the next game. Which bloody idiot had arranged these fixtures?

In the intervening years I have come to love compiling the fixture list. It is an inexact science. All teams are different;

everyone has their own way of doing it. Some people will call me, others will wait to be called, many do it by email, one or two by old-fashioned post (and you suspect they would rather do it by carrier pigeon if they could). Some teams want exactly the same weekend, year in, year out. Then every seven years you shift forward a whole week to restore equilibrium. (The only trouble with this is that no one can ever agree which year it is that everyone shifts forward a week, so you inevitably end up with a huge and terrifying fixture logjam that Stephen Hawking would struggle to unravel.) Other teams hop around the schedule like Mexican jumping beans. One team is constantly disbanding, then reforming, like a progressive rock band from the 1970s. Another will fix a date and then want to change it five or six weeks later. They claim that they have double-booked, but you know that a better fixture has come along and they want that one instead. Everyone has a hierarchy of fixtures. For a travelling team like ours, the hierarchy would run roughly as follows:

Category A: glamorous and/or famous teams; also teams with access to amazingly scenic grounds.

Category B: teams with access to amazingly scenic grounds, but they always beat you and/or the tea isn't much to write home about; also teams you really like but they play on a dungheap; also anyone you always beat.

Category C: teams who always beat you and/or the tea isn't much to write home about, but there's a good pub to go to after the game; also anyone you think you might have a reasonable chance of beating on a good day.

Category D: teams who messed you about last year, or with whom you have had a big row, but who have significant redeeming features (doughnuts at tea/late-opening pub/no bowlers under fifty).

Category Z: the gits and twats. (You obviously don't want to play the gits and twats, especially after what happened last year, but if you suddenly find you have no games at all in July . . .)

For me all this starts in the early new year, as I stare out of the window at leafless trees and huge lumbering thunder-clouds, dreaming of last-ball victories on sun-dappled village greens, and me walking off the field with 85 not out, raising my bat to the eager applause of my team-mates and a coachload of beautiful girls who just happened to stop by to watch. Wonderful. So much better than the real thing. Without blind optimism, though, most cricket teams would cease to exist. Blind optimism fuels the belief that this will be the year. Never mind that all previous years have been a little disappointing. It's this season that counts. So I get on the phone and ring up another fixture secretary, who, as chance will have it, has been staring out of the window thinking exactly the same thing. If we were not psychic, we would not be fixture secretaries.

In theory such calls should only take a couple of minutes. Sort out a date, agree which pub we're meeting in, laugh at how old and infirm all our players are. But there is always more to talk about than that. Which teams have disbanded, which teams have been taken over by outsiders or idiots or snarling youths, the retirement of old So-and-So, the arrest of old So-and-So's son for GBH – this is the stuff and substance of the January phone-round. It's the first sign of spring: the sound of fixture secretaries gossiping.

We are tenacious souls. Like dictators of third-world countries, we hang on to our jobs for dear life. A fixture secretary may complain incessantly of his heavy workload, but it doesn't mean he'll let anyone else do it. In many teams, such as mine, no one else wants to do it, but that doesn't lessen the paranoia. If a fixture secretary is called away on business, he will only hand over his database to someone he regards as no threat at all – his children or, at a stretch, his wife. I once heard a very sad story of a fixture secretary who had to go abroad for six months and delegated fixture responsibilities to his beloved spouse. Unfortunately she was having an affair with one of his team-mates, so when he came back he had lost not only his wife, his children and his house, but also his job as fixture secretary and, consequently, his place in the side. The poor man had to take up fishing.

There is a tricky side to the job, and that is pruning the fixtures your team-mates want rid of. It may be that no one from the other side told their fixture secretary just how disastrous last year's game was. The fist-fight after the disputed run-out was bad enough, but the burnt-out kitbag was a bridge too far. Your team will not play them again and it's up to you to excise them from the list as cleanly as possible. This has only happened to me a couple of times, but my usual solution is to do nothing. With a bit of luck they won't ring you until March or April, by which time you can pretend your only spare weekend is 4/5 October. Or do what someone did to me recently: arrange the fixture as always, then get someone else to ring up six weeks later pretending to be the 'new' fixture secretary and cancel it on transparently spurious grounds. They'll get the message. (I did.) Everyone gets dumped from a fixture list from time to time. In Captain Scott, where tempers invariably ran high, we lost one or two every season. When Harry tried to ring up to arrange a game the following year, the number had suddenly become unobtainable, or, if he did get through, the fixture secretary would pretend to be Hungarian.

We were and are a travelling team, and so easily fobbed off. But it's harder if the team you hate are just round the corner. I know a team who told an old opponent that they had disbanded, simply to avoid having to play them. The fixture secretary had to ask the other teams they played to go along with the ruse, even though the two villages were only ten miles apart and probably shared more than a postcode. What they didn't know was that the detestation was mutual. The other side were delighted they had 'disbanded'. Although, they told me, they did wish they had thought of it first.

4

A FRESH START

Slowly a team comes into being. You have the fixtures, and
some kit, and the crazed determination to find eleven players for each game, or ten, or eight. At first you'll take
absolutely anyone. It doesn't matter if you have never met
them, or they are out on bail for firearms offences. If they are
available, and can walk, they are suitable for your team. It
pays to be broad-minded, because you never know how
new players will turn out. You don't know whether the
team will like them, and whether they will like the team.
Fact is, some new players stick and most don't. We were
lucky in Rain Men, as we had inherited a solid rump of
players from Captain Scott. Terence the Human Sieve,
Howard who can hit an on-drive at will, Neal the dibbly-
dobbly merchant, Cliff the run-out expert and Richard of
the crazed whims: they were all stalwarts, and there were
several others. I managed to coerce most of the players I
wanted to join the new team, and was happy to leave behind

one or two. Any long-running cricket team contains at least a couple of people you don't like much. Captain Scott had contained a lot of people who didn't like each other at all. We had been running each other out and dropping each other's catches for years. Here was an opportunity to start afresh.

And in that first season, 1998, we didn't do at all badly. Of seven games played, we won two, drew two, and the other three I have forgotten about right now. Along the way we witnessed heroic deeds, as previously feeble and decrepit players exceeded all expectations. Chief among them was Neal, who had been batting at number six or seven for years, and had thus become the sort of batsman who makes a quick twenty and gets out. Not that I am decrying such players. I myself dream frequently of being able to make a quick twenty. I wake up bathed in sweat. But Tim the incredibly angry fast bowler has a theory that some batsmen bat according to where they are put in the order. Put them in to open and they become fiercely correct and play out maidens with aplomb. Put them in the middle order and they become swashbuckling; lower middle order and they slog; bottom of the order and they bat as though they have never batted before and never will again. In particular this is the way Tim says he bats, although I have found that wherever I put him in the order he tries to hit a prominent minority of balls over deep mid-wicket's head for six. But Rain Men needed an opening batsman, and Neal volunteered. And quite quickly he became one, acquiring a more than functional forward defensive where before there had been none. He still makes a quick twenty and gets out, but now he looks the part, and that's what matters. That's all that matters in village cricket.

Not that the traditional values of our game were ignored. As the first season's Sad Statistical Digest revealed, we scored more ducks (thirteen) than we took catches (ten). I would like to have included wicketkeeping catches in that last figure, had there been any. In Rain Men it pays to bowl at the stumps, and hope the batsman misses.

Possibly the defining moment of the summer came in our game against the Heartaches, the team of old friends and layabouts run by Sir Tim Rice OM, CH. I was umpiring at the time, and one of our batsmen hit a juicy slow long-hop straight to mid-wicket, who dropped the easiest catch you will ever see.

'Oh bad luck,' said Sir Tim. Several of his team-mates echoed the sentiment. Not a single one threw his cap down in rage and screamed 'Oh for fuck's sake!' before kicking a stump out of the ground and chasing the poor fielder into the pavilion with what lawyers would call 'intent'. Howard, the non-striker, turned to me and said, 'Isn't it nice to play a team who are actually sympathetic when someone drops an easy catch?' It worked, as well. When I came into bat I hit a similarly dozy long-hop to the same fielder, who caught it brilliantly one-handed an inch off the ground.

The most amusing dismissal of the season, though, was suffered by Terence, who after his heroic 30 in the first game had been lobbying me all season to be allowed to open the batting again. So I let him, and he clubbed his first ball through square leg for a safe single. The second run seemed riskier, but he called for it anyway, and was run out by several yards. At the same time the umpire at the bowler's end was calling one short, because Terence, whose eyesight is catastrophically poor, had run his bat into an old crease on the next pitch, which sadly was a yard or two short of the crease on ours. He therefore became the first batsman any of us had ever seen to be run out first ball coming back for a second and still score 0.

New players appeared; most vanished as quickly; one or two stayed. What makes certain people find a cricket team and stick to it? I wish I knew. In our team the one qualification has only ever been willingness to play. My selection system is terribly straightforward: first come, first served. Book early and you get in, no questions asked. If Graham Thorpe rang up and booked in twelfth, he wouldn't get a game. Actually that's not true: I'd probably have one of the first eleven shot. But even then, I'd pretend somebody else had done it. It's more important than anything in my position to be seen to be fair. (Certainly more important than being fair.) For the beauty of this system is that it repays enthusiasm, which as everyone knows is the most precious of all cricketing attributes. The more someone wants to play, the more he or she gets to play. One slightly awkward consequence is that the team thus selected can be crap. Indeed, we have sometimes put out sides so weak you could only identify us as cricketers by the fact that we were wearing white. But at least everyone was there because they wanted to be there.

Indeed, I think this is one of the advantages of running a slightly more elderly team. The players whose hearts were not in it have gone. Which is sad, if you are evangelically minded like me, and you believe that cricket can enhance, if not transform, any person's life. In the past I have been known to blame cricket-hating spouses for the disappearance of fine players into the domestic realm, but – and this may be another consequence of growing older – I no longer believe anyone really does anything other than what they want to do. When you are twenty-five and you have much time and no money and few options, you don't need to be especially dedicated to enjoy a few games of cricket. Twenty years on you might need to be slightly deranged to play at all. And have an understanding wife or girlfriend. Whom you have chosen, without consciously understanding your motives, partly because she would tolerate your continuing need to play cricket. Meaning that, on some level, this game you may once have played just for something to do has come to form the very texture of your life. Everyone needs someone to love – just so long as she doesn't mind a few pairs of pads lying around the place.

The only player in that first game who stuck around was Robin, who is an actor, and whose greatest performances, I believe, have been pretending to be a cricketer. Before I begged him to play he hadn't taken part in a cricket match for twenty-five years. I think he had been put off at school, as so many people are when they find they have no great talent for the game, and had been deterred thereafter by the entirely natural fear of making a fool of himself. Which is strange, as for Rain Men CC he now happily makes a fool of himself on a regular basis. How many other non-players are out there, not realising how much fun they could be having every weekend, batting and bowling and fielding not particularly well? Robin, once he started playing, developed a real taste for it. These days he rarely misses more than a couple of games a year. And yet sometimes I wonder. Why is he so motivated? Like all actors Robin looks terrific at the crease but doesn't score that many runs. His fielding is no worse than anyone else's, but no better either, and his bowling is only an occasional weapon as he chucks the ball blatantly. Why does he play nearly every single game?

Because, as I have discovered, Robin is one of the most competitive games players in Europe. He is an old friend of my girlfriend Polly's and he and his girlfriend often come round to eat food and drink wine. Once, but only once, he brought his mah-jong set round. I had always thought of mah-jong as a rather peaceful, civilised sort of game. And so it is, when not played by Robin. It was as if Steve Waugh had decided that what he wanted, more than anything in the world, was to be the best person in your house at Totopoly. Robin played with brutal precision. When anyone else looked like winning, he cited little-known rules that stopped them winning. He actually had a handbook of these rules, much thumbed. The evening ended in bitter recriminations, and they didn't come round for dinner again for a while. Some months later there was a children's party, and a game of grandmother's footsteps . . . but I'm sure you can imagine that.

Perhaps surprisingly this intense competitive streak does not translate into boorish or aggressive behaviour on the cricket field. Indeed, Robin is the most sporting of players, and sulks only briefly when run out without facing a ball. He is not competing with the rest of us, as he would be when playing mah-jong. I suspect that he is competing against himself, and his upbringing, and the teachers who told him he was no good at cricket, and finally against the game itself. And he won't be beaten. At Ardley-with-Fewcott in our third season, he dived at a ball at mid-off, fell on top of it, and stood up looking very strange indeed. His skin had gone grey and his collarbone appeared to have a step in it, with an inch or so between the top step and the bottom step. It took him the best part of a year to recover. The surgeon said it was a freak injury. Robin waited for it to get better, patiently did his physiotherapy and started playing again the following season as though it had never happened. You have to respect that.

We played seven games in the first year; nine in the second; nine in the third; ten in the fourth. We won a few as well. The team began to develop an identity, as teams tend to. When you are running a team and making what you think are all the most important decisions, you might be tempted to think that this is down to you; but it isn't. When we ran Captain Scott together, what Harry wanted more than anything was a team that essentially did what he wanted. And what I wanted was a quiet life. From the beginning, though, the Scott team attracted a stream of lippy, determined characters, many of whom thrived on conflict, much as flies thrive on shit. A couple were supremely skilled dissemblers, who would maintain their own status by undermining others, both behind their backs and to their faces. One or two were natural courtiers, adept at playing off one side against the other. New players would come along under the impression that they were going to play cricket, and find themselves playing mind games with psychopaths. No wonder so many ran screaming.

To some extent, Rain Men CC came into being as a reaction to this. Again, maybe it's because we are all older and have worked out that there are more important things in the world than someone dropping a catch. But these days there is little tolerance for bowlers throwing huge queeny tantrums. Silent double teapot is accepted from Gloomy Bill, our slow-pitch bowler, who has been found in tests to have no idea that he has adopted the teapot position, single or double. You can't chide someone for an involuntary teapot. And I think we have to allow a little leeway to batsmen who have been outrageously sawn off or otherwise humiliated at the crease. But one notoriously demanding Scott bowler came and played for us, and gave us his full repertoire of theatrical moans and glares whenever anyone fumbled the ball, which was often. In the pub afterwards three players sidled up and expressed a preference that this person never be seen in Rain Men colours again.

Every team acquires its own distinctive personality. And every new person who joins a team adds something of themselves to the whole. It's a little bit like being assimilated by the Borg in *Star Trek*. (Resistance is futile.) All the teams you meet have their own distinctive personalities as well. They are different from you, they are different from each other, and they will be different again next year, because someone else will have arrived or left and changed things further. A team you get on perfectly well with this year may be a bunch of unscrupulous bastards next year. And vice-versa. It's utterly unpredictable.

Our lot are definitely a more peaceful, contented lot than they were. The malicious backbiting has ceased, and when one person does well, the others are now genuinely pleased for him. Recently we brought back none other than Tim the incredibly angry fast bowler, who took several years off to grow some keep-yourself-young facial hair and tend his various injuries. It was a bit of a gamble, as in the old days Tim could single-handedly scupper whole fixtures with one brutal spurt of invective. But he has fitted in well. He still thinks the other side are cheating at every turn, but these days he keeps it to himself. Maybe he has mellowed. He certainly believes so. He says he even plays football less aggressively. He plays five-a-side every week in a group that includes Harry, who Tim says is a 'maniac' on the pitch. A week or two after he told me this I had lunch with Harry, and happened to mention that I thought Tim had mellowed.

'Bollocks,' said Harry. 'You should play football against him. He's an absolute maniac.'

The weird thing is that even Captain Scott has changed. We left partly because we were tired of the infighting. And after we left, the infighting stopped. Funny, that. These days Harry's players are almost all much younger than he is. Many are Australian and South African, who come along recommended by other Australians and South Africans whose visas have run out. (There is a splendid urban myth going around about a cricket captain who, finding he was short a few players, went down to Heathrow, waited for the next plane to come in from Sydney and held up a card saying 'Anyone fancy a game of cricket today?' And was virtually mobbed.) Harry's younger players, he tells me, treat him as a sort of beloved elder statesman, or knackered old family pet. He still bowls hundreds of overs and opens the batting in crabbed and ungainly fashion, but nowadays no one seems to mind. In other words he has a team that essentially do what he wants, while I have a quiet life. When we go out to lunch together, we marvel at what has happened. Neither of us wants to analyse it too closely, in case it all goes horribly wrong.

5

THE CHANGING GAME

It's not just teams that change with the years. The whole
game is constantly mutating, despite many people's apparent
need to pretend that it stays exactly the same. Those books
are still coming out, you know. The ones that hark back to
a golden age of English cricket, before ramblers and 'holiday
homes' and mobile-phone masts were strewn across the
countryside, when indeed there was a countryside, as
opposed to the vast agrochemical expanse interconnected by
motorways that has replaced most of it. Of course cricket
changes. Even in the past ten years you can see the difference. And hear it. And sometimes smell it, if you are on a
municipal pitch and tramps are asleep in the outfield. Cricket
in the twenty-first century challenges every sense organ, as it
probably should.

• Helmets. Ten years ago anyone who went out to bat in a
helmet was a figure of fun. Fielders would try not to laugh,

and usually fail. The wicketkeeper might guide the batsman to the crease as though he were unusually frail, or mentally distressed. Even the batsman at the other end would wear a broad grin, and try to run out his partner at the first opportunity. Fast bowlers would be particularly inspired, reasoning that anyone who worried so much about being hit on the head might have forgotten to install protection over other, equally vulnerable areas of the body. Oddly enough these batsmen all gave the same reason for wearing a helmet: that their cheekbones had at some point been shattered by rising deliveries and that their entire heads were held together with screws, bolts and copper wire. At such a tale all cricketers would gasp with horror, for at heart we are kind and generous people, as well as inordinately gullible.

Not long afterwards the first teenager appeared wearing a helmet. Fielders muttered. Were we that barbaric? No, there had just been a change in the rules, requiring all juniors to wear helmets when batting. All teens would henceforth grow up watching the ball through a metal grille. It's the same way, I imagine, that budgies view the outside world. After that, helmets started to creep into the adult game. One or two village batsmen known to be quite good were using them. The helmet became one of those items of equipment that every team has in its bag. People are known to 'call for a lid' when the pitch is a bit bouncy. We have one, and I have occasionally been tempted by it. I have never played a hook in my life, as I know I would get a top edge straight into my face. A helmet would make this possible. (Actually, a miraculous infusion of talent would make it possible. A helmet would just stop it from being impossible.) But I can't bring myself even to try it on. Partly it's because I always think of *The Man in the Iron Mask*, but mainly it's because old prejudices die hard. Perhaps in ten years' time. Or twenty.

• Pub opening hours. Ten years ago – and it's a shock to recall this – pubs shut on Sunday at two o'clock sharp and opened up for business again at seven. All right, a pub you know didn't and a pub I know didn't, but most stuck to the rules with a respect for the law that verged on the superhuman. Ever since the First World War, when licensing laws had been changed to discourage munition workers from drinking themselves to death when they should have been making weapons for people to blow each other up with, there had been five sorry boozeless hours every Sunday, which may be why so many of us played cricket instead of watching it with foaming pints in our hands. When pubs were finally liberated in the late 1990s, so were village cricketers. Not only could we now have a crafty glug during our batting innings if the pub was close enough, but we were henceforth spared one of the more appalling manifestations of cricket at its lowest level: the beer match.

Think about it. You have just lost to some prancing village team by what seem like thousands of runs or hundreds of wickets. You want to have a shower and a lie-down and then climb into a large glass of beer, followed by another one. These are normal healthy feelings to which you are completely entitled, as a member of a humiliated losing team.

But pubs do not open until seven o'clock. It is now just before six. You have more than an hour to kill. No number of showers will solve this problem. You could always drive home but that would be deemed unfriendly behaviour by the opposition, and they would be right: schmoozing in the boozer afterwards is required of all visiting teams, by ancient cricketing tradition. So the opposing captain suggests a beer match. Ten overs a side, an over each per bowler, a bit of fun before the pub opens. And it will be a bit of fun – for him and his team. He will have the opportunity of letting bowlers bowl and batsmen bat who didn't get a proper chance while your team were imploding. Whereas your lot, tired and miserable, must now go out and lose all over again.

But no longer. Now, just before six o'clock, you and the other captain look at each other and say, beer match? Or go down to the pub? Rather like the game of cricket recently concluded in the other team's favour, it's no contest.

• Sledging. Everyone agrees it's worse. Even the people who do it agree it's worse. The latest thing, intriguingly, is batsmen sledging fielders. Heard last season, one batsman to his partner: 'There's two there. That cunt can't run.' Before we know it, umpires will be seeking the power to send players off. Or give them electric shocks with specially adapted light meters. One for the ECB, I think.

• Sunglasses. Did anyone wear sunglasses on the field of play ten years ago? A handful of Test players did, but they were universally regarded as show-offs. Then the wrap-arounds came in. Impressively expensive and apparently unbreakable, they caught on quickly in village cricket. Before I knew it I had already lost two pairs. When the glare of the July sun is melting your retinas, sunglasses are fantastic, and I can see why Jack Russell always wore them. Then, suddenly, a nasty black cloud blots out the light and you feel like one of those pricks who wear sunglasses indoors at night. Indeed, you're very nearly as likely to come to physical harm, as the first you will know that the ball is flying towards you at deep square leg is when it hits you on the head. If the sunglasses don't get lost en route to casualty, they will be trampled underfoot by whoever fields the ball. Then there's Sunglasses Anxiety, usually experienced by slip fielders as the bowler runs in to bowl. You realise you are not wearing your sunglasses. So where are they? Are they resting on your cap? Have you put them in your pocket? Did you drop them three balls ago when you chased the ball down to third man? By the time you have worked it all out you have dropped more than your sunglasses. Stupid bloody things.

• 'Catch it!' The ball goes up in the air, you are under it, and the bowler shouts 'Catch it!' This is because he has seen people doing it on television, and therefore he believes that it is a thing worth doing. But what else were you planning to do with it? Shoot it down like a pigeon? Donate it to charity? Perhaps he thinks you need to be told to 'Catch it!' so you don't juggle it feebly and then drop it. But, as everyone knows, being told to 'Catch it!' makes you *more likely* to drop it. Better, surely, for the bowler to shout 'Drop it!' because then you might actually catch it. And even if you don't, the batsmen will be so surprised and confused you'll have a very good chance of running one of them out.

• Baseball caps. You can divide village cricketers very neatly into two groups: those who wear baseball caps on the field of play, and those who believe wearing baseball caps on the field of play should be punished by death. There's no obvious solution to this conundrum that doesn't involve genocide. But the first major league baseball player who goes out to bat wearing a Harlequins cap should be offered British citizenship and, at the very least, a CBE.

• 'Humorous' umpiring. It's a close decision (i.e. he can't remember the relevant law). So the umpire makes a TV-replay symbol. Very dull after 50,000th repetition.

• The football hegemony. Strange to think that football was once the winter game and cricket the summer game, and that Chris Balderstone played for Carlisle United and Leicestershire, where he was more properly known as J.C. Balderstone. Even ten years ago the disparity between the sports did not feel overpowering. We knew that cricket had become a minor sport compared to football, but it still counted for something. No longer, of course. Football has become a huge ravening maw, swallowing all the world's money. Sad politicians try and curry favour with a boot-crazed electorate by pretending to have witnessed players score goals who retired before they were born. Sports pages in newspapers are now football pages. Morons fly the flag of St George from their cars during major football tournaments. Children play little else. At the end of a year in which England's cricket team win almost every Test going, the BBC decline even to bid for the TV rights they had previously held for forty years. Football is now more than a rival; it has become the enemy. And Rain Men's best bowlers and batsmen still crock themselves for months at a time playing five-a-side. *It makes me so angry.*

Still, at least no prominent cricketer would be so foolish as to wear an alice band on the field of play. We have nothing else, but at least we have that.

• The rise and rise of cricketing euphemism. Blame television. Ten years ago, when an umpire made a grievous howler in a Test match, Richie Benaud would either say nothing or, with a slight harrumph, 'I'll leave you to make your own minds up about that one.' Now Dermot or Bob or whoever says that so-and-so was 'adjudged lbw' (i.e. it was missing leg stump by six feet and might have hit the square-leg umpire) or 'given out' (i.e. it has come giftwrapped from the umpire and the fielders will be writing thank-you letters after close of play). Everyone knows what they are talking about, but no one spells it out. Why not? For fear of undermining the umpire's authority? You couldn't undermine it any more if you dressed him in a clown's costume and a funny hat. (Which, I hear, may be on the cards for the next World Cup.)

• People talking rubbish generally. Here's Ricky Ponting on the England team (August 2004): 'Some of the individuals have really put their hands up and grown in stature over the last twelve to eighteen months.' Rain Men individuals, by contrast, put their hands up for a split second and hurriedly pull them down again before anyone has noticed. Other beauties include 'crackerjack shot' (© M.C.J. Nicholas), 'coming to the party' (= putting your hand up) and 'stepping up to the plate' (= coming to the party). Or take this from the 2004 C&G final between Gloucs and Worcs. Hussey bowls, Solanki hits the ball straight to a fielder and wicket-keeper Adshead chirps, 'Love a dot, Huss.' Stephen Fleming, the New Zealand captain, has been heard to talk of 'good dotting'. Oh for the days of Jim Laker, and 'he gave that the kitchen sink' . . .

• Sunblock. Like alice bands and Dominic Cork, this has already been and gone. Ten years ago Test cricketers were only just starting to anoint their faces with blobs of white oily stuff extracted from the internal organs of endangered species as soon as the sun came out. Global warming, as well as bringing first-class cricket to Durham, had seemingly changed the face of international cricket for ever. Within a year or two, sunblock had filtered down to village level. Ropey medium pacers with beer bellies were slapping it on like warpaint to give them a bit of 'edge', they said. And for a while batsmen were duly fooled. Any bowler with the guts (or the gut) to look that daft must have something about them. In Rain Men we figured that sunblock alone accounted for half a dozen wickets a season, which nearly made up for the presence of the Human Sieve behind the stumps. Even in April, when heavy cloud cover meant that an Aldis lamp would be of more use than sunblock, batsmen were sufficiently distracted by the sight of it to throw away their wickets more wantonly than usual. Sadly, though, the mystic power of sunblock proved short-lived. Soon everyone was wearing it, and no one was fooled any longer. These days the sun is more powerful than ever and sears through white puffy English flesh like a laser beam, but sunblock seems to have vanished. Nowadays one person brings along a bottle of factor 15 and everyone else 'borrows' it. And several rare varieties of whale breathe easily again.

• One-day fielding. We have all seen it and we all rather admire it, in a crazy break-a-bone-to-save-a-run kind of way. Older players obviously prefer to encourage it from afar, applauding when a younger player dives feet first, hits a muddy patch and slides straight across the boundary into a ditch full of brambles. Rain Men fielders, when called upon to chase leather, tend to do so in the traditional manner: trotting along behind the ball in the hope that it will reach the boundary, which means they wouldn't have to pick it up, turn and hurl it back with all their strength, only to see it go about twenty feet and stop dead. This practice is known in one team we play as 'shepherding', but then fielding has always sorted the sheep from the goats. We know we are the goats. Or the sheep. Whichever is supposed to be worse.

Nonetheless, one-day fielding does often provide unexpected entertainment. Here's one from a recent game. Batsman hits the ball into the offside. Rain Man 1 chases. Rain Man 2, who has a much better throw, is just behind. Rain Man 1 gets there first and flicks the ball up for Rain Man 2 to catch. Unfortunately, he flicks too well. The ball flies high over Rain Man 2's head in a gentle arc. By the time they have sorted it out, a regulation two has become an all-run four.

In the same game our opposition also chose to illustrate some of the perils of one-day fielding. A young fielder was running after the ball down to third man. Flushed with enthusiasm, he dived at the ball feet first, even though it wasn't going for a boundary and he could have just picked it up. At the same moment fine leg was racing around at full pelt. He couldn't stop himself, tripped over his team-mate and went flying. The batsmen ran one more. The diving fielder's excuse: 'There was a huge molehill there.' His captain's response: 'Not any more there isn't.'

• The new fabrics. Once, and not so long ago either, all cricketers wore old-fashioned natural fabrics. Shirts and trousers were made of thick cotton, or something even more traditional that gained weight the more you sweated into it. Boots weighed as much as breezeblocks and even socks had substance. By the end of a boiling hot summer's day you couldn't have been warmer if you had been wearing an overcoat and muffler. And yet for years many of us resisted the new fabrics. Though lightweight and infinitely cheaper, the new shirts and trousers had a plastic sheen that spoke to us of photocopier salesmen and 1970s disco leisurewear. They had logos all over them, and the trousers did up with a drawstring. Whereas my old cotton trousers always shrank after three or four games in the wet, so you didn't need belt or braces to keep them up. On the contrary, you needed a good sturdy pair of scissors to get them off at the end of the game. Had Denis Compton suffered similarly for his art? I do hope so.

I gave in eventually. Polly bought me trousers with drawstrings for Christmas. In some sense that I had been trying for years not to think about, it seemed like the beginning of the end. There's something about elasticated waistbands that cuts to the heart of a fortysomething man's fears about age and infirmity. It's a bit like the first time you hear one of your friends talking seriously about retirement – as though he has been thinking about it a lot, looking forward to it even. Next up, you think, we will wear slippers and have dogs called Rex, and will want nice warm milky drinks before going up the wooden hill to Bedfordshire. All this racing through my mind on Christmas Day, having just unwrapped a new pair of cricket trousers. I was sweating, and my heart was pounding. Fortunately my two-year-old distracted me by throwing his new tractor at my head.

You get used to everything in the end. I love my new fabrics now. They enable me to sweat in a normal fashion, and I don't look anywhere near as much of a pillock as I did in my many doomed pairs of severely shrunken cotton trousers. And who would ever be able to tell that the waistband was elasticated, if you never tuck in your shirt?

• Reverse swing. Yeah. As if.

6

FOR BETTER OR WORSE

Playing on into your forties, as we all seem to be, prompts certain questions. When, and how, will you start getting worse? Will it all fall apart gradually, or very quickly indeed? A sixty-year-old of my acquaintance tells me that the bowling usually goes first. Then the fielding goes. The batting goes last of all, although I would have thought that batting isn't going to get any easier once you have lost the ability to take a quick single. As Neal said after a recent run-out, 'I thought I was running really fast, but it turns out I wasn't.' (If someone translated that into Latin, I think we'd have it as our club motto.) I should also point out that Neal took the second run based on his observation that the fielder was wearing black trousers. How many of us have made that mistake? The boy may not have had the kit, but he did have a throw like an automatic rifle.

The Bowling Goes First

I believe this. After all, in some cases it has already gone. Martin the former fast bowler is one whose decline I was bemoaning ten years ago. For a brief period in the 1980s, Martin was genuinely quick by village standards. He ran in from the boundary rope and grunted menacingly as he let go of the ball. His action was never exactly classic: while he was up in the air for that split second before delivery, his feet would flap back and forth at high speed, like a propeller momentarily taken out of the water. Then there was his famous slower ball. Instead of grimacing and grunting, Martin would approach the crease with a silly grin on his face and, with a completely different action, bowl a slow full toss which, to his amazement, was always hit for four. He had as much guile as Thomas the Tank Engine.

Perhaps we should have seen what was coming. But one of the stranger aspects of youth is that you almost never see what's coming. You spot it briefly in passing and then only look for it properly when it has gone. In his thirties Martin worked hard at his career but sadly not at his bowling. By the age of thirty-three he had become a much slower and less effective version of his twenty-three-year-old self. Everyone tried to persuade him that, by consciously slowing down and practising a few different deliveries, he could become the bowler we needed him to be. But Martin wasn't having it. In his mind he was a fast bowler: strong and tough, with a grunt like Monica Seles. By 1995 he was already reduced to second change, brought on at the end of an innings to scare the young and inexperienced. Every year he would bowl one really good spell, which made everyone's eyes light up. But he had no idea how he had done it. Next game he would be back to normal and hating every second of it. I felt sorry for him but didn't know what to do. So I wrote an extremely blunt assessment of his bowling in *Rain Men* to try and provoke him into action. With anyone else in the world this might have worked.

Ten years on Martin plays less and less often and bowls less and less effectively when he does play. In the meantime he has improved as a batsman, and can come in at number six and flay quite decent bowling to all parts. But his heart isn't in it. My guess is that if his heart was in it, he wouldn't be able to do it. His heart is in fast bowling, in running in at full pelt, in pulling horrible faces at the batsman, of leaping in the air and waggling his feet to no known effect. Sadly the rest of his body refuses to co-operate. He keeps pushing himself to do something he is simply unable to do any more. And he is so stubborn he won't admit it to himself, let alone hear it from anyone else. He is our friend and we are all fond of him. But what on earth do we do?

So far, though, Martin is the only bowler who has lost it completely. Most of the others have adapted their game, or were never so good in the first place that you would notice any decline. If it's already broke, don't fix it.

Then the Fielding Goes

It's in the field that, as a team, we seem most vulnerable. Six or seven years ago I vividly remember Charlie Dinnerparty, who is famed for always leaving matches early to go to a dinner party (having arrived late after a lunch party), running for a ball through what appeared at first glance to be treacle, but may just have been a heavy crude-oil spill. You know those dreams you have in which you are running as fast as you can but you don't move an inch? That was Charlie as he valiantly tried to catch up with the speeding ball, which, unlike him, didn't sit at a desk all week. His limbs were whirling with the effort. His teeth were clenched. And his cries of despair could have been heard half a mile away. But the actual distance he covered was negligible. 'Too many dinner parties,' we all crowed. The poor bugger was only thirty-three. Little did we know that we were seeing all our futures that day.

Now, in our forties, we are each acquiring our own specific frailties. Some players can barely run; many can barely throw; and Martin has long since stopped trying to bend over. You might as well ask the Forth Bridge to field the ball. As captain I try to be sensitive, but sometimes it's a struggle. After a while you give up trying to hide certain people in the field, because there's nowhere you can hide all nine of them. According to Robin the actor, the worst thing now is to be asked to save the single. The batsman hits the ball straight at you, you pick it up, throw it in, but he's taken the single anyway. So you come in a few yards. He does the same thing. You come in further. He does it again. Sooner or later, feeling victimised, you field the ball cleanly and try and buzz it in at full speed, but you throw it so high and wide that it goes for four overthrows. A quick single has thus been transformed into a throat-slashing five. Robin thinks we should stop trying to save the single altogether and just concentrate on keeping them down to four.

But it's all relative. Last season, on a tediously sunny Saturday when we had no game, I took my children up to the local green space where there happened to be (i) an ice-cream van, and (ii) a cricket match going on, thus killing all conceivable birds with one stone. As my loved ones inhaled their Strawberry Mivvis, and dimwit blokes kicked a football around in the outfield, I watched the cricket, which was between two teams of teenagers. It was fascinating. The bowling, though swift, was deliciously inaccurate. The batting was a delight. Several of these boys could really play. Then, like everyone in our team, they would get themselves out idiotically. Clearly this is not something you learn, it's something you are born with.

Then there was the fielding. These boys were astoundingly quick across the outfield. They dived about feet first, saving certain fours, and threw the ball in to the wicketkeeper with amazing power. (Did we once do that? I couldn't remember.) The wicketkeeper would then fumble it. Useless wicketkeeper, I thought. Watching more, though, I realised he was no worse than anyone else. Although they ran and retrieved well, their ground-fielding was hopeless. When the ball was hit at them, they fumbled everything, even the easiest balls. And they scarcely ever took a catch. It slowly dawned on me that these kids were every bit as rubbish as we now are, but *in completely different ways.* They had vast reserves of energy, which enabled them to run around all day like antelopes on wildlife documentaries. But they had no guile, no experience. We have decades of experience and so much guile you could bottle it. Our ground-fielding isn't bad these days, if only because no fielder wants to have to run all that way if he misses the ball first time. That's the fruit of experience. We have learned that as youth recedes, so does the boundary rope.

Ground-fielding has also become more important because none of us can throw any more. This means that a particularly long boundary can easily turn fielding into a relay event. I find this terribly embarrassing. When Howard or someone shouts 'Help him with the throw!', the batsman is immediately alerted to the fact that the fielder who has gone after the ball can only throw it a few feet, and the other fielder who has gone to help him can only throw it a few feet as well, because otherwise he would have gone all the way out there and thrown it all the way back himself. My sixty-year-old friend told me there is worse to come. 'What?' I said. I couldn't imagine anything worse. 'When you need *three* fielders to get the ball back. That's worse.'

The Batting Goes Last of All

Again, this is relative. Nasser Hussain felt he was losing it at the age of thirty-six while Graham Gooch started to look vulnerable at forty-two. But they were usually playing against the top half-dozen bowlers in the world. We occasionally play against the bottom half-dozen. Batting skills at our level tend to be undimmed by middle age. I have been trying to persuade an old friend of mine to play for years, but he is completely cycling-crazed and rarely out of lycra. And he says all the usual things: haven't played for ten years, totally out of practice, don't want to make a fool of myself, don't want to let anyone down. Last year I finally wore down his resistance, and he turned up for the last game of the season. He took a good catch in the deep, which was a start. Where would he like to bat? Oh, low down, nine or ten will do. So I put him at number six, and the third ball he received he effortlessly flicked off his legs for four. I have played every weekend for the past twenty years and I can't do that. He was good. He *is* good. It doesn't matter that he didn't play for ten years. If you have got it, you generally keep it. Indeed, one of the best batsmen we play against is in his mid-fifties. He has no backlift to speak of and is on the portly side of prosperously well padded. And we still can't get him out. There is hope for everyone.

For there is the chance, slight but identifiable, that a batsman might not get worse with age: he might actually get *better.* I have to admit that the chance is greater if you weren't much good to start with. Indeed, the more pathetic you are, the more enormous is the potential for improvement. In this sense, if in no other, youth is in the mind. Nasser, at thirty-six, was already so old in his head when he retired that he called twenty-seven-year-old Andrew Strauss a 'youngster' – not once, but a recorded 6,293 times on Sky Sports. But Nasser had been a very good player. At his age, he was never going to get any better. At my age, though, I might. So might Robin our actor. So might several other Rain Men, despite the fact that we are all over forty and rarely practise in any way at all, so as to keep ourselves physically fresh and mentally uncluttered for the big day.

Here's a heartwarming story. It tells of Simon R, so called because, give or take a few letters, that's his name. Simon never used to play cricket, had never knowingly let the concept enter his head. He led an entirely different life centred around freelance journalism and the fleshpots of central London. (You like him already, don't you?) Then, one day in our second season, I asked him if he felt like making up the numbers that weekend for the Rain Men.

'But I'm useless,' said Simon.

'Everyone says that,' said I.

'But I really am hopeless,' said Simon. 'I've never played the game and I was always last to be chosen for all games at school. Even after the fat boy.'

'Never mind,' said I. 'You are now forty-one. These things don't matter any more. Anyway, we are a mixed-ability side. In Rain Men former internationals rub shoulders with children, old folk and men with one leg.'

'That's not quite true, is it,' said Simon.

'No,' said I. 'No former or current international has ever played for us. But you'll love it. Nice people, no pressure. There might even be some girls there.'

(It was the day before the match and I was desperate.)

So Simon came and played. He wore not-quite-cricket kit, misfielded countless balls in the deep, faced three balls for 0, and asked when he could play again. Would there be girls next week? Well, it was always possible, I said, my fingers crossed behind my back.

And over the next couple of years, despite seeing even fewer girls than he scored runs, Simon became a regular. He didn't bowl and he fielded like an arthritic gimp, but he fitted in and we all liked him. There was something about his relentless gloom that cheered us all up. For him the glass wasn't half full or half empty. It was completely empty, and it was someone else's glass anyway. He bought some cricket kit and asked people to bowl at him in the nets. Though rooted to the crease like a small tree, he occasionally made a run. Once he and Gloomy Bill put on 104 for the sixth wicket: this remains our team's record. Simon's share was 7, his highest score.

I think this may have been when it all changed for him. Until then he had never watched cricket, or talked about it, or remembered any of the field placings. I think it was just something to get him out of the house on Sundays. But then we began to hear stories of his practice sessions. He'd go on holiday and force his brother-in-law to bowl at him all day. He became increasingly frantic if he had to miss a game. He started watching it on TV, and asking people technical questions they couldn't answer.

Fast forward to 2002. In his first three games of the season, Simon scored 2, 2 and 2. He was having no trouble getting off the mark. The second single usually came easily as well. But then he froze. We'd see the wild swish, the clatter of bails, the sorry walk back to the pavilion. Simon decided he had to do something about it. He rang Surrey CCC and booked up some coaching and a bowling machine. For hours he toiled in the nets at Guildford, practising the forward defensive. The following week he looked a different player. He kept on asking me to put him up the order, so I did, and when it was his turn he almost sprinted to the crease. With shots all around the wicket, he looked a powerhouse of determination and confidence. Until a few balls later, when he was out for 2.

Simon's story does not end here. But his almost superhuman determination shows that anyone can improve their game, especially from a standing start. The rest of us gain encouragement from his development, slow and expensive though it has so far turned out to be. But hey – if we weren't unnaturally patient we wouldn't be playing cricket. Ten years ago my lifetime batting average was a whisker under 4.2. Now, after an outrageous number of not-outs, it's a smidgen over 5. If I can get it to 7 before I keel over, I'll die a happy man.

The Future

The point is that, at whatever age you play, there are bene-
fits and there are disadvantages. Most Rain Men are barely
halfway through the Seven Ages of Cricketer.

Age 1: Tyro. Excellent at running around very quickly,
less good at bowling and batting stuff. If in a team with
grown-ups, much shorter than everyone else. If in a
team with contemporaries, still forced to play with
tyros who show real talent but haven't yet moved up to
a higher echelon of the game. Either way, you can't
win. But you can wear a helmet. This is the Age of
Promise and Parental Pressure.

Age 2: Young adulthood. May now be playing cricket
because there's nothing else to do, and it's cheap. Still
good at running around. Getting better at
batting/bowling. Slightly disturbed that girls not much
interested in you in your whites. Haven't yet realised
that they never will be. This is the Age of Energy and
Self-Delusion.

Age 3: Your prime. Cricket has seeped into your
bones. You cannot escape it now. Speed around the
boundary now less important than ability to pace an
innings and bowl a tidy spell at the death. If not
actually captaining, constantly suggesting changes of

bowling and field placings to captain, hoping he'll retire and let you do it. Girlfriend/wife may not like you playing twice every weekend. First visit to DIY store at around this time. This is the Age of Impending Doom.

Age 4: Stalwart. Girlfriend/wife has given up trying to stop you playing, or left you for someone else. You are the backbone of your team. Unfortunately you wrenched all your back muscles this morning and are unable to move. This is the Age of Physiotherapy.

Age 5: Veteran. You always field in the slips. Bowling has slowed right down. Batting crabbed but effective. Have taken on some form of club responsibility – captain, groundsman, fixture secretary, treasurer – to make it harder for them to get rid of you. This is the Age of Consolidation and Slow Decline.

Age 6: Ancient. Can only justify your place in the side if you are really good at what you do, or if it's your team. If spin bowler, feared by everyone. Very rarely field at deep mid-wicket. This is the Age of Hanging On By Your Fingertips.

Age 7: Freak. If you last out the entire game without dying, someone calls the *Ten O'Clock News*.

7

THE JOY OF STATS

Is it strange to know your current lifetime batting average to two decimal places? I discussed this with Richard, Rain Men's other registered statistical obsessive. We agreed that three decimal places was a bit much, while four was certifiable, but two was perfectly normal, and only knowing your lifetime batting average to one decimal place was a bit lax, if we were to be honest.

Nonetheless, some players claim not to be interested in statistics – even their own. They include some otherwise estimable international cricketers, who drivel on in interviews about it being the result that matters, and they want to do their best for their country, and they don't care how many runs they have scored or at what average, as long as the team is winning and they are doing a job for the team. Oh shut up. Pull the other one. Steve Waugh never said anything so daft. Whenever he was batting with the tail, you could always see in his eyes the fierce determination not to get out before the other guy. That average was dragged screaming up to 50 and stayed there ever after. Except for a few Tests, towards the end of his career, when it dropped to 49 or even 48 and Waugh began to look vulnerable. He knew that history judges you on your statistics. Dragging that average back past 50 again may have been his greatest achievement as a player. Captaining sixteen Test victories on the trot? Pah, anyone can do that.

For many of us, to know cricket statistics is to love them. (Hence Bill Frindall's legendary success 'with the ladies'.) I was in a pub in Muswell Hill the other day with my friend Chris, when he said, 'Do you know who that is?', pointing at this substantial bloke at the other end of the bar surrounded by lovelies. Before I could say 'It's not Bill Frindall, is it?' he said, 'It's a New Zealand cricketer. Can't remember his name, but that's his sister with him.' I swiftly identified the cricketer as Daryl Tuffey (and the sister, accordingly, as Daryl Tuffey's sister). At which moment the following sentence also came out of my mouth: 'Yes, he's taken sixty-odd wickets at about 28.' I checked this later, and it was about right. So which was sadder? That I knew it, or that I checked it later?

It is a mania, possibly a disease. Thank heavens for the mighty Wisden organisation, which can now keep all our statistical urgings fully sated. We can buy statistics from them in book form. We can download them from the internet. Or we can have them delivered to our homes by men in green overalls, who also take away our old statistics for recycling. All without a prescription. It is quite miraculous.

In Captain Scott, it pains me to admit, we never particularly went a bundle on stats. Harry would produce a statistical digest at the end of the season and that was it, really. As he had played all the games, and opened the batting in every game and bowled by far the most overs, he had usually scored more runs than anyone and taken more wickets than anyone, which obviously eroded everyone's enthusiasm a little. My main priority was not coming last in the batting averages. I always managed it, sometimes by the slimmest of margins. For this I could usually thank my good friends and fellow bunnies Terence and Stephen, as well as Harry's girlfriend of the time, who used to play regularly, much encouraged by me. But as the years went by and my keenness waned, so did any glimmer of interest in the stats. In the late 1990s Harry undertook a root-and-branch reappraisal of the club statistics, which meant going through every page of every scorebook and adding everything up again. But I was no longer willing to argue about which games counted as 'games' for the records, and whether 'retired' should mean 'retired out' or 'retired not out'. I no longer cared. I said as much to Polly, who was delighted. 'The day you no longer care about cricket statistics', she pronounced, 'is the first day of the rest of your life.' Thanks a bundle, sweetie.

Anyway, it was only a temporary lapse. After Rain Men CC's third match I produced our first ever Sad Statistical Digest, and have updated it after every match since. This modest, double-sided sheet of A4 contains the latest batting and bowling averages, as well as specific statistics relevant to the match just gone. Did someone hold on to a catch? Then there's a full list of the season's catch-takers, and maybe an all-time list as well. Did someone concede 20 runs in an over? Then there's a list of the half-dozen most expensive overs we have ever conceded. (The record is currently 23, shared by Neal vs Thebertons in '98, Richard vs Charlton-on-Otmoor in '03 and Francis the stockbroker vs Brook Strollers in '04. Like Bob Beamon's long jump, this is a record no one seems to be able to break. We keep thinking a 24 is on its way, but opposition batsmen keep letting us down.)

You can see how this would suck you in, can't you?

Initially I just printed off a couple of copies of the Sad Stats for everyone to pore over at the next game. Then one or two players asked if I might fax the latest edition over to them at work some time during the week. Now – hooray for technology – I send a pdf by email to twenty-five crazed stats-heads mid-morning on Monday. Sometimes I am a few hours late, because I have been compelled to do some real work for money. People then email me to ask me why I haven't sent it yet. (These tend to be the people who have recently scored runs or taken wickets. Serial duck scorers are altogether more patient.) At the end of the season I expand the document to eight mouthwatering pages. I suspect that one or two people only come to the end-of-season drinks to be sure of grabbing a copy.

There is a limit, sadly, to the sort of statistics I can compile. We are not one of those teams that has its own dedicated scoring person, who turns up and keeps the sort of records that aliens will unearth centuries hence and recognise instantly as the work of intelligent and civilised lifeforms. I meet a few scorers from time to time, and as well as being impressed by the huge number of different-coloured pens they own, I am always struck by the deep, loving precision of their work – which, let's not forget, records entirely inconsequential friendly cricket matches played by middle-aged men who need an excuse to get out of the house. Real scorers calculate the number of balls every batsman faces, they time an innings down to its last second and they know the right symbol for everything. We are less rigorous. Our scorer tends to be the only person who vaguely knows how to do it and who isn't already batting or umpiring. Some of our scorers forget to record the fall of wicket, and virtually none can make all the figures add up at the end. But there's usually enough information to keep the Sad Stats monster fed, which is all that matters.

The next step, everyone tells me, is the website. A few teams we know have succumbed to this particular lure, which at least gives you somewhere to put all your stats and match reports and photos of each other being bowled middle stump. Technology is the statistician's friend. At first. Soon, it is the statistician's master. Servicing the website can take up time otherwise reserved for earning a living, seeing your family or playing the occasional game of cricket. The other day a friend of a friend offered to set one up for me at a very good price, and was quite surprised when I started waving garlic at him and attempting to drive a stake through his heart. You have to resist such temptations for as long as you can. I am taking it one day at a time.

There is no end to what you can do with stats if you have the time, the money and the inclination. For his team the Heartaches, Tim Rice produces an annual pocket-sized paperback handbook full of match reports, photos and statistics. Of course he is vastly rich and can afford to, but, having received and read a few of these annuals, I know that if I were vastly rich I would do exactly the same thing. His statistics are wonderfully baroque, and mesmerising in their total meaninglessness. In our Sad Stats I record the number of 50s ever scored by various individuals (not very many). Tim has the most individual 50+ scores, the most individual 50+ scores in a season, the most individual 25+ scores, the highest individual score on debut . . . One of my favourites, and one I intend to plagiarise as soon as I have the time, is most runs in a month. February's just happens to be M.C.J. Nicholas (Hants and Channel 4) – 185 runs at 37 in 1992–3 – but most of the records have been set by the ordinary, non-celeb players who make up 95 per cent of the team. And virtually none of them have been set by Tim himself, other than the ones for Turning Up Most Often. This is my kind of cricketer.

Harry, my old confrère in Captain Scott, has gone one stage further than this, as you would expect. For the team's twentieth anniversary in 1999, he had privately printed a complete *Wisden*-like almanack, complete with yellow dustcover and 864 pages of solid drivel. It had match reports for every game, many depressing photos of us all looking young and singly chinned, and millions upon millions of statistics. Few psychiatrists would require more evidence than this to have him locked away and plugged into the National Grid for the rest of his days. We laughed at his mania, and all bought copies at £60 a throw. Some of us smuggled them home so our wives and girlfriends wouldn't see them. Mere ownership of the book might have undermined these relationships permanently. Finding out how much we had coughed up for the privilege might have provoked divorce proceedings. At least one former Scott player wrapped his copy in a real *Wisden* dust-cover to draw fire. But then most wives and girlfriends probably don't realise that *Wisden* itself now costs £36 – money that could be more wisely spent on food for our babies, or indeed anything at all.

All this requires a specific mindset. If you were the only person in your team whose thoughts travelled along these lines, you might become a little lonely. But let's face it, it's not very likely, is it? Football hooligans like hitting people, Conservative MPs like wearing slightly seedy pinstripe suits, cricket fans like to know why Leicestershire wicketkeeper Tom Sidwell's dismissal against Surrey at the Oval in 1921 remains unique. (He was the only first-class cricketer ever given out after getting lost on the London Underground.) Whatever else is going on in your life, however incident-packed it may be, some part of your brain is always reserved for such thoughts. Sometimes it's a fairly substantial part of your brain.

In 2001 we played the Screaming Blue Warthogs, a tough outfit from the mean streets of Bicester. (Actually they are just as useless as we are, but I find it helps to talk up your opposition, especially in the pub before the game.) On a sunny afternoon and a typical council pitch – moribund but occasionally prone to extreme violence – I foolishly elected to bat, and we were soon 36 for seven. A devilish bespectacled fast bowler had taken most of them. Somehow our tail managed a recovery, led by Simon, who accumulated 6 in sixteen overs. Going in at number eleven, I top-scored with 11 not out. (It was our first game of the season, so I thought this might be the start of something big. It wasn't.) By this stage the devilish bespectacled fast bowler had finished his spell. The Warthogs' captain had sportingly insisted on a maximum of eight overs per bowler, despite the fact that he had no one else who could bowl. Hooray for sportingly! We made 69 in the end.

To make a game of it, they reversed their batting order, and were soon 24 for two. An incoming umpire told us that Dominic Cork had just taken a wicket in the Test match. I wandered up to Richard and, to avoid talking about the game we were about to lose, I asked him whether he could think of any way of getting out in international cricket that had fewer letters than 'b Cork'. Richard immediately suggested 'b Vaas' as a tie. Vaas remains one of his favourite cricketers, mainly because he is the only one he can think of who has more initials (W. P. U. J. C.) than letters in his surname. He also has a sneaking regard for the New Zealand bowler Heath Davis, who played five Tests in the mid-1990s. Although he usually goes in the scorebook as H. T. Davis, the T stands for Te-Ihi-O-Te-Rangi, a Maori god. (There is a belief that the praying mantis is his material manifestation.) Richard prefers to believe that this gives him six initials, which breaks all records.★

While we discussed all this, Warthog wickets began to fall.

'How about "b Lee"?' said Richard.

The match was becoming tense.

'Or in the 1970s you could have had "b Old",' said Richard.

Our bowlers, all closely related to the donkey, were suddenly bowling like thoroughbreds, and we were taking catches all around the wicket. The Warthogs collapsed to 42 all out. We had won. We couldn't believe it.

But Richard was now thinking of the longest way you could be out in first-class cricket. 'How about "c Ingleby-Mackenzie b Sivaramakrishnan"? If they'd ever played together, which obviously they didn't. Thirty-four letters excluding the hyphen.' His mind had picked up the baton, run round the track with it and straight out of the stadium. If he had registered our victory at all, it was only at the very edge of his perception.

★ More recently, Sri Lankan domestic cricket has been adorned by the all-round performances of A. R. R. A. P. W. R. K. B. Amunugama. He hasn't yet played Test cricket, but Richard and I would be rooting for him if he did.

I mentioned this sequence of events in a column that happened to have my email address printed at the bottom of it. I should have known. Instantly some of the nation's finest cricketing minds sprang into action. For weeks the debate raged. First there was the matter of titles to resolve. If they were allowable then 'c HE The Maharaj Kumar of Vizianagram b The Rt Hon. Lord Home of the Hirsel' (fifty-nine characters) would surely have broken all records, had it not been for the fact that (i) these two never played together, (ii) Lord Home of the Hirsel was then plain Viscount Dunglass, and (iii) it was all too silly for words.

I therefore decided to restrict the debate to combinations that might actually have occurred. The man who developed the Deloitte ratings thought the longest Test dismissal of all time might have been 'Bromley-Davenport c Fichardt b Middleton 26' at Port Elizabeth in 1896. (It wasn't, but it had a music all of its own.) He also suggested that the most meagre contribution for the most number of letters might have been that of P. S. 'Percy' Twentyman-Jones, who in his only Test in 1902 made two ducks and didn't bowl.

My favourite contribution, though, came from a man who signed his email as 'Mike Turner (scorer)'. Mike believed a record of sorts had been set in the 1982–3 series between West Indies and India. In the fourth Test at Bridgetown, *Wisden* recorded both Larry Gomes and Clive Lloyd as being out 'c sub (L. Sivaramakrishnan) b Venkataraghavan'. That's thirty-seven characters apiece – thirty-nine if you count the brackets. As Mike wrote, the true glory of these dismissals lay not just in the length of the names, nor in the fact that a substitute had been involved. 'No, the icing on the cake is the character L, which is vital in differentiating Laxman – not being a member of the Test XI – from any other passing Sivaramakrishnan who might have strolled on to the field that day and taken two substitute catches.'

By this stage my eyes were beginning to swivel in their sockets.

Several weeks afterwards, at Ardley-with-Fewcott, with all thoughts of the extended Sivaramakrishnan family forgotten, I brought Richard on to bowl his flighty googlies. This can be a risk, but as ever at Ardley it was a wicket of cruel spit and bounce, and today was Richard's day. With his first ball he induced the batsman to leap up the track, flail madly, miss and be stumped.

And then the next ball he did exactly the same thing.

0.2–0–0–2.

Hat-trick ball.

Any normal bowler would have been gambolling around with delight and *joie de vivre*.

But no. Richard was looking thoughtful. He was contemplating hat-tricks. To be precise, he was contemplating hat-tricks of stumpings. Or, to be agonisingly precise, he was trying to remember the name of the only first-class cricketer ever to take a hat-trick of stumpings.

Did anyone else know?

We shook our heads. Richard trudged back to his mark.

Everyone edged in for the hat-trick ball, but I knew the game was up. Richard had been distracted at the crucial moment. Even if he remembered the man's name he'd want to know his initials. Sure enough, the next ball was a hopeless long-hop which the new batsman bludgeoned past point (M. Berkmann) for four.

Richard emailed me the following morning. He had looked it up. The only first-class cricketer ever to take a hat-trick of stumpings was W.H. Brain, off the bowling of C.L. Townsend for Gloucestershire against Somerset at Cheltenham in 1893. Which, for some reason, I now remember and will always remember, until I am ninety-five and gaga and whispering to the nurses, 'W.H. Brain off the bowling of C.L. Townsend for Gloucestershire against Somerset in 1893. Oh yes, I remember it well.'

There are probably worse ways to go.

8

THE OPPOSITION

Who are they, these strange people you meet once a year on the field of play? It's an axiom of village cricket that you pay more attention to your own team than the people you're playing, as it's within your own team that all the most diverting undercurrents and overcurrents will flow. It doesn't matter who on the other side is bowling, when the umpire, who is on your side and hasn't yet batted, is gagging for an opportunity to give you out, and the other batsman is so jittery he may run you out any moment anyway. In international cricket coaches and captains and players study videotapes of their opponents and construct intricate plans on how to deal with them. Whereas we go into bat and think, oh there's a fat man bowling. So we go up to the non-striker, who happens to be Cliff, and we ask him, what's the bowler doing? And Cliff says, haven't a clue mate, we had a party of video editors in at the bar last night and I'm so tired I can barely stand. Sadly, John Buchanan and his piecharts would be wasted on us.

Fortunately, in my dual role as non-winning captain and fixtures supremo, I have a fair amount of contact with the opposition. Indeed, some of our regular opponents have turned into good friends, and one or two have even been enticed to come and play for us when they are at a loose end. There are certainly two I have known for more than twenty years. The near absurdity of these bonds – people you speak to once a year to arrange the fixture, and see once a year when you play the fixture – is, oddly, the source of their strength, which may be true of cricket friendships as a whole. With cricket friends and cricket acquaintances you are freed from the drab necessity to talk about the vicissitudes of daily life, and can simply concentrate on the one subject that binds you all together. Women think men are mad and sad for doing this, which is exactly the opposite of the truth. Long inconsequential conversations about Ashley Giles's resemblance to a wheelie bin keep us sane and happy. And seeing the same faces at cricket matches year after year is, for me, one of the main pleasures of playing. The last thing you want to hear is that someone you have known for years has retired. And when they have died of old age: well, who gave them the right to do that?

For most of our players, though, opponents drift by in a bit of a blur. At the same time we are all drifting by in a bit of a blur for our opponents, and the fact that you all go to the pub afterwards makes things even blurrier. Sometimes when I am droning on to someone in the pub afterwards I suddenly wonder, did I have this exact same conversation with him last year? Or was it someone else last week? You don't dare ask.

'Sorry, this may sound strange, but have I said all this before at some point?'

'Yes. About twenty minutes ago.'

Repetition, though, is the essence of bar talk. For the past couple of years, wherever two or three cricket fans have gathered together, probability has approached certainty that one or other of them would tell the Eddo Brandes and Glenn McGrath story. Only on the 110th repetition does this story begin to pall, unless you're Glenn McGrath or, more worryingly, Mrs McGrath. Or more worryingly still, any of Mrs McGrath's many English relatives, who are probably out there waiting with knives for someone stupid enough to tell them the Eddo Brandes/Glenn McGrath story.

For some players it's a problem, knowing what to say to the opposition. At the start of a post-match drink, teams tend to congregate in separate packs, like teenagers at a school disco. But a travelling team needs to maintain good relations with its hosts, and this generally means that conversation must be broached. But what if such matey pub chat does not come easily to you? What if you become rigid with fear that you might say the wrong thing?

Things to Say to a Member of the Opposition in the Pub after a Match

- 'Fantastic tea, that. Some of the tastiest sandwiches I've ever eaten.'
- 'Beautiful ground. So well looked after.' (WARNING: Only say this if ground is beautiful and well looked after.)
- 'Well bowled. Were my eyes deceiving me or were you getting a little late movement through the air?' (WARNING: Be careful who you say this to. It doesn't matter whether or not they bowled well, let alone gained a little late movement through the air. All that's important is that they bowled at all.)
- 'What are you drinking? Can I buy you another one?'

Things Not to Say to a Member of the Opposition in the Pub after the Match

- 'Was that your daughter doing the teas? Blimey, what a dog.'
- 'So tell me, when was the last time anyone in your village gave someone out lbw? Before the war?'
- 'You know that catch I claimed low down at slip? Took it on the half-volley. Yeah, thought you'd laugh.'
- 'I don't mind you beating us. It's the way you stole all our kit that really pissed me off.'
- 'Has anyone ever told you that you smell faintly of cheese?'

You will find it surprisingly easy not to say any of these things if you put your mind to it. (Putting your mind to it may be the tricky bit.)

As I said, most of the teams we play are our friends and we love them almost carnally. (They will cancel our fixture if I don't say that.) But everyone knows of teams who don't play in the requisite spirit, that mess you about, play mind games, piss you off. We in non-competitive village cricket are lucky. We don't have to play anyone we don't want to. But if you play in a league you may come up against one of these teams year after year after year until . . . what? Violent retribution? It seems a little drastic. But I know of teams that have resigned from leagues in order to avoid having to play a particular side they hate. There's nothing else you can do. For most of us life is just too short for a full-blooded feud, unless you have excellent links with organised crime.

Here, then, are a few varieties of annoying, irritating or merely frustrating opponents. There may be hundreds more.

Team 1: Run by an Arse

This team are as amiable as can be: they're friendly before, during and after the match and, although they usually beat you, they do so in good spirit. All of them, that is, except their captain, who is a prize arse. Never stops talking, constantly heckling from the sidelines. Needlessly offensive to the opposition at all times. Convinced you are cheating when you aren't. Then comes out to umpire and himself cheats blatantly. When fielding, sledges all batsmen, even though this is a Sunday game and there is nothing at stake. Bowls beamers and doesn't apologise. The rest of his team shrug their shoulders. 'Sorry, he's always like that,' one or two of them tell you after the game. But secretly that's the way they like him. Because he's like that, it allows the rest of them to be gracious and polite, and that absolves their consciences while they beat you hollow. Ten Mr Nices and one Mr Nasty. It's clever.

Team 2: Friendly off the Field, Bastards on It

Great fun in the pub beforehand. Then on an evil council pitch, two six-foot-four-inch fast bowlers bowl bouncers for over after over, while close fielders chirp aggressively, and there's no change of bowling even when you are 23 for eight. Then they are as friendly as ever in the pub afterwards, although you feel less inclined to chat matily than you did before. This type of team are always absolutely astonished when you don't want to play them again the following year.

Team 3: Random Malevolence

This lot are famously awkward. There's the Smiling Assassin, who is charm personified, but cannot resist ending each sentence with a nasty little quip. There is The Man With

The Eyebrows, who is always looking for trouble. When two or three of this team are gathered together, chances are they are looking at you as though you just tried to steal their cars. But their captain is a lovely bloke, who somehow manages to keep a lid on his team-mates' aggression. What could be an impossible fixture is rendered playable because of him. Then one year you turn up and the captain isn't there. Maybe he is injured, or has sensibly moved to another part of the country. And suddenly the rest of the team's random malevolence is unleashed. The Man With The Eyebrows takes over as captain, and your fixture turns into one of the more epic battle scenes from *Lord of the Rings*. They try every trick in the book, and several not yet written down. And when you respond in any way to their stratagems, they respond further with seething resentment, which allows them to occupy the moral high ground. You can't win with this team – which naturally is the idea. If only I'd held on to that catch at third man! If only I hadn't left my bat in the changing room, never to be seen again! (Note to lawyers: this team is totally imaginary and none of these things ever happened.)

Team 4: The Weather Aliens

Some games are just cursed. Sometimes the weather is against you, and sometimes aliens have invaded the village and only want to play cricket against you in order to harvest your bodies afterwards for your internal organs. At this fixture I believe both circumstances applied. I had had terrible problems with numbers, and by the time someone had pulled out with a rollerblading injury – another first for us – we were down to a pitiful seven. I rang the opposition captain and, with some embarrassment, cancelled. The forecast was for persistent rain after two o'clock. It seemed the most sensible thing to do.

But the opposition captain disagreed. Ten minutes later he rang back. He had found some extra players. Did we fancy ten-a-side? Well of course we didn't, but you can't say that, so I rang everybody up again and we drove off to our doom. The rain began at 1.47 pm. As we arrived at the ground, it was bucketing down.

'Ready to go then?' asked the opposition captain, who was already changed.

'Hadn't we better wait for the rain to stop?' I asked.

'Ah, what's a little rain?' he yelled, as lightning struck a nearby house. At three o'clock, with third man deep under water, we announced we were leaving. They couldn't understand. Admittedly, their eyes were now glittering with a silvery sheen, and Terence was certain that their wicket-keeper had an extra set of teeth. We drove off in close convoy, never to return.

Team 5: The Chocolate-Box Village

Let's call it Chuffington Magna. By some miracle you have managed to get a fixture there. Chuffington Magna is one of those magnificent English villages whose many murders are generally solved by Miss Marple. Film crews are everywhere, litter is punishable by death and you'd have to sell an orifice to afford lunch at the local pub. People creep out at midnight and comb their lawns. You know the sort of place. Just about its only saving grace is a perfect village green, on which a team of killer stockbrokers regularly trounces visiting opposition. Someone you know once played there and said it was fantastic. It didn't matter that you wanted to shoot everyone there in cold blood, he said. If you play there once, you want to play there again.

And somehow this prize fixture has landed in your lap. There's no need to explain how it happened. Someone has talked to someone, who has consulted someone else, who has talked to someone else, who has given you the all-clear. Rupert the fixtures stockbroker has been in touch and a date has been set. You spend the intervening months boasting about the game to everyone you meet and waving your fixture list in their face. And on the day you and your team turn up in very, very clean whites, with sandwiches because the Michelin-starred 'pub' has been booked out since February. You meet your opponents. They are a little cool.

In one or two cases, very cool.

You wonder. You cogitate. Have any of your players misbehaved? Hardly: they haven't yet had the opportunity, and are all grossly sober. Are you scruffy? Do you talk in the wrong accents? Do you drive the wrong cars? Very probably, but do any of these things really matter?

Then it dawns on you. You have a black player in the team. And an Asian player. It is, after all, the twenty-first century, and you have never shown the slightest inclination to invade Poland. But in Chuffington Magna there are no black people, there are no Asian people. Even a Frenchman would do well to escape unharmed. Two or three of their players are giving you hostile looks and muttering under their breath. You won't be asked back. You wouldn't come back if asked. Now all you have to do is get through the game and get out of there.

And spread the word.

9

INBOX

From: Simon
To: Marcus
Date: Thursday, September 6, 2001, 11:49 pm
Subject: Depressing stuff

Dear Marcus,
Looking forward to Saturday. I did sustain a severe paper
cut yesterday but, with adequate medical attention, I hope
to be fit for the day, weather permitting . . .

From: Simon
To: Marcus
Date: Monday, August 5, 2002, 11:41 pm
Subject: Bollocks

I'm practising madly here.* My brother-in-law has been working hard on my elbows, eyes, hands and so on and for the first time ever I've managed a few cover drives and whatever those ones are when it's bowled outside leg stump and you have to hit it behind you.

Can't believe Sept 7th is the next time I'll play unless Legionnaire's disease hits some of those who have committed to play on Saturday.**

From: Simon
To: Marcus
Date: Wednesday, August 7, 2002, 3:12 pm
Subject: Weirdness

* On holiday in the Peak District.
** Originally, Simon did not put himself down for this game as it was right in the middle of his holiday. The game was to be played at Stonor Park, on the Oxon/Bucks border. Then he changed his mind. But by then thirteen people had booked ahead of him. A couple of people still had to drop out if he was to get a game

Coaching Connie★★★ madly. Been practising cover drives today and getting better. Cannot do an on-drive for love nor money. Getting very irritated.

Incredibly stiff from the unaccustomed exercise. Steve my brother-in-law has even shown me how to bowl but I've pulled something in my side getting overenthusiastic . . .

Connie's showing some promise and Steve's son Jack (just eleven) would probably be an asset to our team the way we're playing at the moment.

Keeping my fingers crossed that a mild form of bubonic plague will hit some of the waverers before Stonor.

From: Marcus
To: Simon
Date: Wednesday, August 7, 2002, 8:25 pm
Subject: Re: Weirdness

Someone else has just dropped out of the game on Saturday. There's a space for you. Interested?

★★★ Daughter, aged seven.

From: Simon
To: Marcus
Date: Wednesday, August 7, 2002, 11:28 pm
Subject: Re: Re: Weirdness

I'd probably have to set off now to get there but I'd like to nonetheless. It would be so staggeringly pointless (especially if I get a duck) that it HAS to be worth doing.

I have to check and doublecheck a couple of things. Apart from staggering distance I didn't bring any shoes or trousers or shirt. I need to have a look in wardrobe. I can probably play in t-shirt and creamy trousers but I have no tennis/trainer-type shoes. If Jane★ doesn't veto it I might go into Chesterfield to buy some spikes . . .

From: Simon
To: Marcus
Date: Saturday, August 10, 2002, 7:12 pm
Subject: Bugger

★ His wife.

98

Not surprisingly, I'm a little bitter. Because we didn't get to play I KNOW I'd have done brilliantly and not been bowled out for a golden duck by my former boss as would almost certainly have happened if we had played.★★

In fact the only thing that made today bearable was the fact that a guest arrived who'd been on a week's cricket course and who was happy to keep bowling at me. So, fully padded up, new spiked shoes on, and wearing gloves, I have been doing forward defensives, cover drives and even the odd attempted on-drive and sweep. The fact that he's only ten years old and using a training ball is totally irrelevant.

I wish you could see how I've been playing this past week as I'm sure by September 7th I'll have forgotten everything I've been taught and there will be no sign of any improvement. Such a shame the next fixture is so far away. Why do we have to stop in mid-September? How am I supposed to last until next May? I've even taken to watching some of the Test and can now recognise occasional shots and fielding positions. You've ruined my life, Marcus. I hope you realise that.

P.S. Do you clean the base of cricket shoes or just leave all the gunge to fall off next time?

★★ The game had been called off that morning, but not before Simon had set off down the motorway. Fortunately I managed to reach him on his mobile before he drove more than twenty-five or thirty miles.

From: Simon
To: Marcus
Date: Monday, August 12, 2002, 8:55 am
Subject: Officially now a saddo

Just realised I've been standing in front of the telly with a bat in hand trying to copy Alec Stewart's position.

From never watching cricket to this appallingly sad situation in just a year. What have you done to me, you bastard?

10

SURVIVING THE WINTER

The cricket season is cruelly brief. Although the first-class boys start shivering through fixtures in mid-April, we in Rain Men have always fought shy of playing in winter, and really only kick off in mid-May. With a last, sorry, chilly fixture on the third weekend in September, that means a season of about four months – or, if you are a fixtures secretary, nineteen weekends. It's not a lot. Simon has a point. How are we supposed to get through the endless, yawning winter months? At least squirrels can go to sleep, curled up in hollows clutching their precious nuts. We are spared this consolation, and so must find other ways of frittering away the dead time. Some of these ways are remarkably expensive.

(Note that, although time goes between 256 and 512 times faster when you are in your mid-forties than when you were twenty, the close season goes just as slowly as ever. This is because your awareness that you only have a few seasons left *actually slows time down,* and so nullifies the normal accelerating-time effects of encroaching age. Neither the Special nor the General Theories of Relativity take this into account: a crucial omission.)

Time-Killer 1: Follow the Fortunes of the England Team

Not so many years ago this would have occupied just a few weeks of the close season, as England (or even MCC) went off on their one tour of the winter, played a few up-country games, a handful of Test matches and a few one-day internationals and came home again. All very civilised. Some years they even found time to hang around in nightclubs and strafe each other from light aircraft. Not that we ever saw any of this, of course. We read about it in newspapers and listened to it on the radio if we were lucky. In those days, the other side of the world really did seem as though it was on the other side of the world.

Not any more. These days the England team have barely lost the nineteenth of the summer's one-day internationals before they are off on a plane somewhere to lose a handful more. If they really behave, they might be given a four-week break before or after the English season, or maybe even during it. And no one needs to read newspapers any more to find out what happened, because we have all stayed up all night watching it on Sky Sports.

Is there too much Test cricket? If you ask me, there isn't

enough. When one series ends, I find myself flicking madly through Ceefax in search of another one. Who are Australia beating today? Which long-haul flight might Zimbabwe be on? Who are Pakistan's latest opening batsmen and New Zealand's latest opening bowlers? And, most crucially of all, which lucky team are playing Bangladesh? It's all part of the mad merry-go-round that is international cricket, and we wouldn't have it any other way.

Watching it all on Sky, though, has its disadvantages. One is that it costs so much you might find your house and all your belongings being repossessed. Even if you are a millionaire without dependants or any need to work, there is still the Bob Willis problem. Listening to Bob Willis droning querulously on for months at a time is simply not good for you. Add Ian Botham's increasingly bad-tempered they're-not-as-good-as-I-used-to-be opinions and the same ads for cars repeated forty-five times a day and you could be just a millimetre from breaking point. And that's before Charles Colville has popped up on screen with his unfeasibly bouncy hair. No one can withstand that.

So last winter I decided I could do without Sky Sports. We were rather short of funds at the time and this was my way of reducing household expenditure. I rang the cable TV company and asked them to switch it off. I also instructed them that, if I rang up again and begged them to switch it on again, they should refuse. We saved hundreds of pounds and several vicious family arguments, although my children did wonder what that writing was on the television all the time.

'Daddy's watching Ceefax,' said Polly.

'What's Ceefax?' said my daughter.

'Very sad indeed,' said Polly.

'Shh. Thorpey's just been out,' said I. His name, so gleamingly, preciously white for so long, had just turned deathly blue. Whenever anything particularly gripping was happening, I would trot up to the convenience store at the top of the road. The Indian family who run it often watch cricket on their CCTV screens, while teenagers nick yogurts undetected. And very, very occasionally, when everyone was out and I felt I could risk coming back smelling of beer and fags, I would nip into my local pub and watch the cricket there, if by some miracle it was on. Pubs, after all, are for watching football in, and if there's a Fourth Division match being repeated from last night, or Croatia vs Turkmenistan Under-21s live from Split, that clearly has precedence over the deciding Ashes Test. The landlord also likes to watch *Countdown*. Why on earth had I cancelled Sky? I must have been mad. The cable company bravely followed my initial instructions, although I think I may now be officially classed as a Difficult Customer, or even an Arsehole.

Time Killer 2: Follow the England Team in Person

This is the luxury option. I have never done it, mainly because when I was younger and had cash to spare, people didn't do it in the way they do now and, to be frank, it never occurred to me. And since it has occurred to me, I have had family and no money and so haven't been able to do it. I see the ads in the cricket magazines and I gnash my teeth until my gums bleed. Think about it: just a few thousand pounds to be able to watch cricket in distant parts in the company of people you don't know who wear identical t-shirts and chant daft slogans all day, and the whole thing run by an ex-Test player who'd rather be somewhere, anywhere else. I know I must do this at least once in my life, ideally without sacrificing my happy domestic existence or any significant internal organs.

The even dafter alternative is to set up a cricket tour of your own. We'll discuss this later in, I'm afraid, rather appalling detail.

Time Killer 3: Read All About It

Sadly these are not the best days for cricket publishing. Mention the words 'Dickie' and 'Bird' to any publisher of cricket books and they will weep uncontrollably. I myself was given two copies of *Dickie Bird's Favourite Pies* the year it came out, and three copies of *More Favourite Pies* the year after. I'm told that the man who published these retired to the South of France, vowing never to watch a game of cricket again – although I'm not sure he had ever watched one before, either. Certainly it is thought that only the selling-off of school sports pitches has done more than Dickie

Bird's books to undermine the game in urban areas. Henry Blofeld and his bowties have since taken up the challenge to destroy it altogether.

Still, if you can't play cricket, you might as well read about it. Like many cricket fans I seem to have shelves and shelves of books on the subject. The reference books, most of them now out of date. The novelty Christmas books. The Pavilion Library reprints of 1930s classics (which look so beautiful on the shelf you want to stroke them). The tour diaries. The sad autobiographies. Tons and tons of sad auto-biographies. Have I really read all these? Have the winters really been that long?

You could take some of the sad autobiographies to second-hand bookshops, but they probably they wouldn't want them. They usually have a whole shelf of them already. Jack Simmons's *Flat Jack* (1986). Derek Underwood's *Beating the Bat* (1975). Ray Illingworth published three, which tell a tale in themselves: *Yorkshire and Back* (1980), *The Tempestuous Years* (1987) and *One-Man Committee* (1996). Sir Geoffrey Boycott has published six books in all, as many as Charlotte, Emily and Anne Brontë combined. (And which of them scored a Test hundred at Lord's?) Every cricketer writes one in the end, tempted by the substantial sums one or two of them have earned. Apparently it was the publication of *Boycott: The Autobiography* in 1987 that first made Sir Geoffrey genuinely rich. Nowadays he's so loaded, each of his houses has its own corridor of uncertainty.

But what do you call your autobiography? Boycott,

Gower and Imran Khan plumped for *The Autobiography*. Botham, Gooch and Allan Lamb chose *My Autobiography*. More modestly, Allan Border called his mid-career 1986 book *An Autobiography*. Then there was Richie Benaud's ironic *Anything But an Autobiography*, which was anything but a revealing read.

Otherwise there is the deep dark descent into the fiery hell of puns. Alan Knott's *It's Knott Cricket*. Bob Willis's *Lasting the Pace*. Dominic Cork's *Uncorked*. Graeme Hick and Graham Dilley published one about their time together at Worcestershire. They called it *Hick 'n' Dilley Circus*. Hick also wins the award for the most self-regarding title, *My Early Life* having previously been used by Winston Churchill.

Like selectorial disasters, terrible titles for cricket books are nothing new. Godfrey Evans called his *The Gloves Are Off*. Roy Gilchrist tempted fate with *Hit Me for Six*. Mike Denness went for *I Declare*. Three years later Basil D'Oliveira chose *Time to Declare*. No points for the Indian opening batsman who wrote *Sunny Days*. Some books span the generations, and the Pennines. Sir Geoffrey's 1980 book was called *Opening Up*, and so was Michael Atherton's autobiography in 2003. Even Vic Marks couldn't resist calling his *Marks Out of XI*.

There. A whole afternoon spent staring at my bookshelves when I could have been thinking about cricket. We'll get through this winter yet.

Time Killer 4: Read *Wisden* from End to End

Of Cadbury's Creme Eggs it has often been asked: 'How do you eat yours?' Of *Wisden Cricketers' Almanack* it might usefully be asked: 'How do you read yours?' This is how I read mine:

(i) Brief flick-through while sitting on park bench after leaving bookshop. This can take up to three hours.

(ii) Serious perusal during unexpected lull in normal work schedule (or 'unemployment' as we freelances call it). This is when you read the Editor's Notes, sift through the Test match reports, goggle at the averages and compare the Records Section with last year's Records Section. Don't pull that face. You do it as well.

(iii) Final definitive read-through from beginning to end. I used to earmark this for the first Test of the summer in which the opposition won the toss and scored 500, while England's bowlers looked as though they would never take another wicket in their lives. (The first Test of the summer, in other words.) But, what with one thing and another, I have been a little short of time over the past couple of summers, so have managed to save this task up until the close season, which I now realise is its natural home. Only when there is *absolutely nothing else to do* would most people outside Notts and Leics consider reading the report of a Notts vs Leics 45-over match, which is why it is best saved until there is absolutely nothing else to do, for then you might quite enjoy it. The same goes for much of the rest of *Wisden*'s 5,693 pages. Before you are even halfway through them, it's spring.

There are hazards, though. Back in 1997, when I was a mere pup of thirty-seven, I rifled through the Register of Current Players to see how many of them were older than me. The register includes everyone who played English (or Welsh) first-class cricket the previous summer and everyone who played first-class cricket anywhere else in the world the season before. This means it can be anything up to eighteen months out of date, which suited my purposes admirably.

In 1997 I counted forty-eight active cricketers who were older than me. A buffer zone, if you like, in that it was a zone full of buffers. A year later it was down to thirty-three and by 1999 it had plummeted to seventeen: Mike Gatting was still in the list, even though he had retired. Raman Lamba was still in the list, even though he was dead. In 2000 the seventeen had shrunk to nine and in 2001 to six. They were: Eldine Baptiste, Graham Gooch (who had played for MCC against New Zealand the previous year), Peter Hartley, Pat Symcox, Kepler Wessels and a Pakistani I had never heard of called Iqbal Sikandar. I had high hopes of Iqbal Sikandar, who sounded wily and gnarled and might keep playing for another couple of years. But I was to be disappointed. In 2002 the list was reduced to Eldine Baptiste. How must it feel to be, officially, the oldest first-class cricketer in the world? The following year I knew. Eldine had finally retired and the mantle had passed to Kim Barnett. Although he is as bald as an egg and bats like a goose, he is three days younger than me.

So that's 1997 to 2003 – seven years of hell I put myself through for no reason at all. Just be careful.

Time Killer 5: Get Fit

Yes indeed, you could be out on the road, jogging your guts out, tautening your muscles and incurring all manner of unpleasant injury. So what's the point of that? By 'get fit', I naturally mean wait for your various niggles and injuries to heal. I don't mean go out and get some more.

Winter is the season for physiotherapy, for osteopathy and for minor operations you are not sure you want to tell anyone about. Winter is when Neal has his now annual knee operation, which never quite works. By next summer it should have got better, but it never has. He will then play through the pain for another season in readiness for the following winter's operation. Needless to say it's a football injury. The only upside is that it has stopped Neal playing football for good, which has therefore reduced his chance of crocking himself yet further.

For most injuries, of course, doctors prescribe rest. This means a genuine and valid excuse to put your feet up indefinitely (assuming the injury is in the vicinity of the foot, i.e. somewhere below the neck). It's vital not to exacerbate whatever strain or twinge you have been carrying, so no lugging heavy objects around or moving quickly in any direction. Instead, lots of lying on the sofa snoring gently through *Holby City*. You know it makes sense.

Time Killer 6: Equipment

During the summer Rain Men kit is transferred from bag to bag, car boot to car boot, shed to shed, and always with a grumbling reluctance that regrets somebody else isn't doing this. I do everything else, but I'm not having the kit. My flat is too small and the kit is too smelly. In August I swear you can hear it sizzle. These days we divide it among three different bags, and sometimes three different people have possession of those three different bags. Richard is official kit monitor, but he doesn't play every game. Since his purchase of a midlife-crisis convertible, there's only room for a pair of batting gloves in his boot, and one bag will fit into the passenger seat, if there isn't a passenger there already. So the kits floats about. Some of it gets lost. Lots of it gets lost, to be frank.

In autumn, when the various bags have found their way back to him, like salmon swimming home to spawn, Richard does his annual kit audit. This reveals that we now have more pairs of left-handed batting gloves than we started the season with, and four single, unmatching right-handed batting gloves. We have acquired one bat from a team we have never played (a team we did play must have acquired it from them and inadvertently passed it on). And something very strange is happening to the wicketkeeping innards, something that will mean that they have to be replaced, and maybe also a discreet phone call to Porton Down.

So Richard does his kit audit and rings me up to tell me the bad news. Actually it's not bad news, because cricket equipment, though wholly uninteresting during the cricket season, becomes fascinating during the close season. If we are missing items, they must be replaced. Richard used to do this himself, but recently one of the big internet-cum-mail-order firms has moved its main shop and storage facility round the corner from me. There is a God after all.

Robin the actor rings up. Like all men he needs a reason to make a phone call, so I do not believe him when he says he has only rung 'for a chat'. It emerges that he has heard that I am going to the cricket shop in the next few days and could he come along? I say yes. I had been planning to go alone and fondle the new bats myself, but it may appear less pervy if I am accompanied by another consenting adult. It doesn't. It's only a cricket shop, but the two of us feel like a couple of grunty teenagers venturing into a Soho porn emporium for the first time. We are frighteningly furtive. We dare not ask if we can strap on some pads in case they call the police.

But we are saved. Someone else comes in. He is about twenty and frighteningly confident. He tries about eight bats, none of which is quite right. Ah, we say to each other, this is the way to do it. We play immaculate forward defensives with £150 bats for hours, but can't make our minds up about anything and leave having bought only a new scorebook. Terribly sorry, we say to the long-suffering woman overseeing our non-purchases, but we'll be back next week. And the week after that, and the week after that . . .

Time Killer 7: Coaching and Nets

Different teams have different attitudes towards nets. Ours is a sort of a distant respect. We acknowledge that they can be useful, and we admire those who knuckle down and practise properly in the winter months, but tragically we never quite get round to doing it ourselves. Sometimes I'm on the top deck of a bus passing Lord's cricket ground and I think, oh yes, the MCC Indoor School, I remember that. Captain Scott used to have half a dozen nets there before the beginning of every season. Either two people would turn up, or twelve. I can't even bowl in the nets so I always felt slightly uncomfortable: the Man Who Only Wants to Bat. And such practice as I did have never helped much. You play on those fast, true indoor wickets for a few weeks, begin to get into some sort of touch, then go out on to May's pudding pitches, play the shot 423 years before the ball reaches the bat, spoon it up to mid-off and stomp off in the usual rage. Utterly pointless. Either I gave up nets or nets gave me up, I can't remember; or maybe we reached a mutual decision to part and issued a press release to that end. Sometimes I have a tinge of regret, especially when it's mid-June and I still haven't scored a run worthy of the name. Perhaps next year, I think – for I am the prince of procrastination, the king of cop-outs. Thank God everyone else in the team is the same.

Well, not everyone. After his surge of practice in 2002, Simon decided that the 2002–3 close season was time to get serious. Barely had the last game been lost than he was at the Oval, facing a bowling machine fuelled by a kindly but bemused coach. Our end-of-season drinks were in October; Simon was late because he was busy practising. He kept asking me if I wanted to go, and I did, sort of. But I never quite went. I needed time to recover. Simon found a worthy companion in an Australian friend, John Hondros. John had played for us once the previous season, after Simon had introduced him with the sentence 'He went to school with Kim Hughes.' Naturally we were impressed. My brother went to school with Phil Tufnell, but it doesn't make him a spin bowler. (Although, like Tufnell, he's a very talented smoker.) John's solitary innings lasted but a solitary ball, before he was sawn off lbw by an umpire we replaced at the end of the over. Relatively new to these islands, he felt he needed to acclimatise properly before coming and playing regularly, so he and Simon had weekly nets for the best part of seven months, always with a coach and sometimes with a bowling machine as well. I tried to explain to John that the only way he needed to acclimatise was to bring a vest, two sweaters and thermal long johns for the first game of the season, but he may have spent too much time in Simon's company by then.

Still, better to play cricket in a net than to play no cricket at all. Cruelly, his job removed John for the entire 2003 season: he didn't play a single game. As for Simon, his scores were b Brackley 5; b Candy 0; c&b Howard 3; b Osborne 0; run out 2; b Lowe 4; c unnamed mid-off b Scoon 0; st unnamed wicketkeeper b Gazzard 0; b Jones 7; b Kingdom 1; b 'Chris' 0. Admittedly, the 7 against the Gents XI included his first-ever boundary, a thick outside edge that raced away on a fast August pitch. But how much had he paid for each of these 22 runs (@1.83)? And as he had averaged 2 the previous season, wouldn't he have scored them anyway? I had no answer to his questions, although I had noticed that he was failing with more panache now, and better technique. If that was any consolation. Which it wasn't.

Conclusion

As Simon's experience shows, the long winter wait may not actually be worth it. Which is why you might as well keep occupied. In summer, there will be no escape.

11

HORRIBILISSIMUS

We should have seen the signs, for the signs were there to be seen. In 2002 our team score had been Won 4, Drawn 0, Lost 8: not an embarrassment, but nothing to boast about either. Like England, our victories had usually been by the narrowest of margins, while our defeats had been cataclysmic and humiliating. Two of our spinners had got the yips, which no known quantity of lunchtime lager could cure. One of our opening bowlers, AJ, had eaten all the pies. Howard, our on-drive specialist, had looked as good as ever but had kept getting out for 7. Another long-serving, run-scoring batsman had faded out of the picture completely, having grown tired of driving all over the south-east of England. He had signed up instead for his local village team, which played opposite his house. I couldn't blame him, although obviously I felt terribly betrayed. He still rings up from time to time to tell me it's not half as much fun. I hold the phone away from my mouth so he can't hear my teeth grinding. I still hope to lure him back. Players that good are not easily replaced.

What we had also lost in 2002, besides mobility, form, confidence and one of our two best batsmen, was our killer instinct – that vital ability, needed at all levels of cricket, to finish off the opposition with a single decisive thrust. It may surprise you to hear that we ever had any killer instinct at all, and I have to admit I almost feel like a fraud writing the words down. And yet occasionally the chance had come to shut out the other team completely and, as a team, we had taken it, without a second's doubt or hesitation. I never knew I possessed a ruthless streak, although during a particularly commanding early victory a team-mate did suggest that I had started to breathe like Darth Vader. Oh, for a light sabre at that moment. Or some Strepsils. No team, I told him, is useless on purpose. Most of us have uselessness thrust upon us. And Rain Men enjoy winning as much as anyone else.

In 2002, though, a subtle change had come over our performances. Call it complacency, or loss of bottle. Call it creeping senescence. One of the problems with complacency is that you become too complacent to notice that you have become complacent. As yet the wheels had not fallen off, but the axles were shaky, the tyres were flat and the suspension was completely buggered. We were just about roadworthy, but our chances of passing the next MOT were receding by the week.

Take our game against our old friends the Screaming Blue

Warthogs. On another sadistic council pitch we had amassed 94 for nine from thirty overs. It didn't seem a bad score. Tendulkar would only have made 160 or so. Still, the Warthogs were bullish. You could tell by the arm exercises and the Robin Smith eye-blinks as their opening pair walked out to bat that they considered this target within their capabilities. And at 14 for one things were clearly going their way. More so, perhaps, than at 22 for nine. I love it when this happens. Nine times out of ten, of course, it happens to us. But it's just as much fun when it happens to someone else. Not that there was any pressing reason for it. We didn't bowl any better than usual. Their batsmen just kept coming and going, as though they had trains to catch. Neal took four for 5 in four overs. He would have had five for 5 if I hadn't dropped a skier at mid-wicket. Plip! And out. Never mind, we all thought, they've only got 35 for nine. Won't make any difference.

And then the score started to mount. I love it when this happens. Actually, I don't. With characteristic Oxfordshire cunning, the Warthogs had messed with their order again. Their number nine, accordingly, was their best batsman. The ball started disappearing in all directions. We became ragged. Tempers frayed. At the start of the last over the Warthogs were 88 for nine. I brought back my old friend Gags, who has long been our steadiest bowler. Miraculously he kept the runs down. Last ball: they needed three to win, two to tie. Number nine creamed it to me at mid-on. Even more miraculously, I fielded the ball cleanly and threw it back to the bowler. We had won by one run. Relief. Delight. Recriminations. In the pub afterwards the Warthogs were elated, never having expected to come so close. We were morose and grumpy. At the crucial moment, at 35 for nine, when we had had the chance to finish off the game and record a serious victory, we had fluffed it. I had fluffed it. I had shown all the ruthlessness of a Teletubby. From Darth Vader to Tinky Winky: it didn't seem like much of a progression to me.

There had been positives to be gained from the season, as football managers would say. One had been the regular participation of Howard and AJ's friend Conrad, who only has one leg. You may disagree, but I have found that there's nothing that puts the wind up the opposition quite like the clunk of cricket ball on prosthetic leg. We often take wickets immediately after Conrad has fielded the ball in this fashion. Maybe I should mention it to the opposition captain before the start of the game, but for some reason it keeps slipping my mind. I also derive immense satisfaction from the knowledge that, whenever Conrad is playing, we as a team possess an odd number of limbs. Nice bloke, too – although, as you can imagine, not a great fan of the quick single.

There had also been the promise of our youth policy, in the shape of twelve-year-old Nathan, who had played once for us towards the end of 2002. He had fielded superbly and bowled steadily, watched by his adoring jailbait girlfriend, which had made everyone terribly jealous. At the time I had written, 'Next year he will be thirteen and better, while we will all be forty-three and worse.' And so it came to pass. For 2003 Nathan joined a proper club who had nets every week and didn't all split their trousers during the first game of the season because it was the first time they had put them on since the previous September. 'Aren't we good enough for him?' asked someone. Stupid question.

Instead, I recruited a few more ruins in their forties and fifties, and Sam, our new youth policy, because he was only thirty-five. Instantly popular for his willingness to open the batting, Sam also impressed everyone with the uncommon authority of his forward defensive. Tall and determined, he would lurch down the pitch at least six inches further than any of the rest of us would have dared. Sometimes you thought he could almost smell the ball, especially if it was a short-pitched delivery he really should have played back to. The only other real flaw in his game was an inability to score runs. We welcomed him like a long-lost brother.

So, as Loyd Grossman used to say, let's look at the evidence. Good players disappearing, to be replaced by not-quite-so-good players. A flattering victories-to-defeats ratio the previous season. General age-related decline. Simon's intensive winter coaching sessions. These were the ingredients for a truly catastrophic season. Brimming with unjustified optimism, I had arranged more fixtures for 2003 than ever before. The long-term weather forecast was magnificent. There was no way out.

Any team can lose a cricket match. Turn up with eight

players, none of whom can bat, bowl or field, and chances are you will be mauled alive. But say you are trying to win. Say you nearly always show up with eleven, some of whom haven't played too badly in the past. Say you have certain fixtures you know you should be able to win. Somehow, some time, you should be able to cobble together some sort of victory. Shouldn't you? Shouldn't you?

This year the Warthogs game was rained off. Another of our favourite teams – i.e. one we had a chance of beating – cancelled their game the night before because they could not raise a side. Their captain rang from the pub. He's a nice bloke too, and probably felt the need to gargle a few down before he made the call. A third favourite team hung on for a wriggly draw, as one of our players turned out for the other side and blocked for an hour and a quarter. But in most games we were simply blown away. Our final analysis for 2003 was Played 15, Won 0, Drawn 2, Lost 13.

Statistics rarely tell the whole truth. But this one does. God it was awful. We just got worse and worse. By June it was hard to imagine how we were ever going to win again. A team of septuagenarians could have wiped the floor with us. We were everybody's bunnies. Small fluffy tails spontaneously started to grow at the end of our spines. Our body language was awful as well: something like Albanian, or possibly Basque. Bowlers begged not to be brought on, begged not to be kept on, and frequently dropped to their knees in tears if I suggested bringing them back for a second spell. Catches became harder than ever to hold on to. There were eleven men out there, and twenty-two hands apparently covered with soap.

Meanwhile I was having my best season for years. I did actually hold on to some catches, and three times with the bat I managed double figures. This was three times more than in any of the previous three seasons. I also played the best shot I have ever played. Admittedly, it was off the last ball of a limited-overs match we had already lost. And the bowler was eleven. In circumstances like these, as Marx once said, you have nothing to lose but your not-out. I am not renowned for my cover driving, much as I am not renowned for my cordon-bleu cooking or my heavyweight boxing. But the eleven-year-old floated one up outside off-stump and Plok! I hit it so sweetly I wasn't sure I had hit it at all. It went over the boundary before I had taken more than a couple of paces. *It was the sort of shot other people play.* As Gideon Haigh, another club cricketer of modest abilities, once wrote, 'I believe I get more value from cricket than, say, Mark Waugh. He expects to hit the ball where he intends; for me there remains the enchantment of surprise.' We had been pulverised by the unstoppable might of Tusmore Park, but I didn't care a bit. The Rain Men were morose and grumpy in the pub that evening as well, with one unspeakably sunny exception.

It is strange to be prospering personally in a failing team. For one thing it reveals to within two decimal places your precise value to the team: absolutely nothing. I was captaining as well of course, but, though uncharacteristically confident myself, I seemed incapable of motivating anyone else. True, we had a couple of apparently unsolvable structural weaknesses. We lacked an opening bowler. Sometimes we lacked two. AJ, who had eaten all the pies the previous year, claimed to have adhered rigidly to a pie-free diet throughout the winter, but his loss of pace appeared to be permanent. Match-winning second-string bowlers, I now discovered, became cannon fodder as opening bowlers. One or two looked more likely to be struck by lightning than take a wicket.

And our batsmen kept getting out. What can you do about this? You mess with the batting order; you ensure that no one with a grudge is allowed to umpire; you encourage and wheedle and coax. Then you give up and let them get on with it. Simon wasn't the only batsperson to enjoy a horror trot. Robin the actor and even Sam the youth policy endured endless strings of low scores. After a while you begin to spot the signs.

Batsman Full of Confidence

- Strides to the crease with head held high.

- Swings bat around to loosen muscles and plays glorious off-drives to imaginary half-volleys.

Batsman Struggling Horribly

- Shambles to the crease with head held so low it's almost falling off.

- Swings bat around to loosen arm muscles, bat flies out of hand and lands on head.

- Stands up straight at crease, looks imperiously round at fielders, adjusts gloves before facing first ball.

- Hunches at crease like spider, tries not to cry, adjusts gloves before facing first ball, realises not wearing gloves, races off to find some.

- Caresses first ball for four.

- Edges ball through slips for first run after twenty minutes. Then stung by wasp halfway up the pitch and run out in ignominy.

Between us we managed forty-four ducks that season in fifteen games. Compare that to twenty-two catches (and one freakish stumping). If you averaged 8.33 with the bat, you were in the top half of the averages. Only Howard averaged over 20. No regular bowler averaged less than 27 with the ball. My favourite statistic was the number of opposing batsmen we ran out. None. On TV every day we see sharp-heeled young internationals aiming at one stump and hitting. The Rain Men could have had twenty-seven stumps set out in the shape of a Catherine wheel and still missed.

One game in August proved crucial. We had lost several in a row – pride and a desire not to jump off tall buildings prevent me from looking up exactly how many – and we were playing a pumped-up media team somewhere in the home counties. Over two or three previous fixtures we had never quite hit it off with this team. I can't really say why, although their occasional reliance on ringers from nearby leagues when their regulars were on holiday didn't help. Maybe it's that some combinations of teams simply don't click. There had never been anything remotely resembling bad blood between us, but nor had we invited each other round to our houses for tea.

And yet again I lost the toss on a baking hot day on a flat pitch with few bowlers worthy of the description and two and a half gruelling hours scheduled before tea. It's at times like this that you begin to get even the smallest hint of what it must have been like for Michael Atherton to captain England. He had to do it day after day after day for several years. No wonder he was so irritable in the press conferences afterwards.

I got cross at a slightly more awkward moment. Poor Neal, who normally bowls second-change (or first-change at a pinch), had to open from the Scary Woodland end, and was in the process of being demolished. He did take a wicket, to general amazement. But then this big fellow came in, swaggering Viv-like to the crease, and hit fours and sixes and fours and sixes. And I thought, What is the fucking point of all this? Why am I fucking bothering? I started ranting to myself at mid-off, mumbling violently about the unfairness of it all. To be honest we had taken greater hammerings than this, and would again (see the Introduction to this book). But there was something about the height of those sixes, and the swagger of the batsman, and . . . well, I lost it.

Fortunately – and this I put down to my fear of physical violence – there wasn't a comprehensive evacuation of toys from the pram. I didn't shout at anyone or indeed confront anyone. I am a coward, with a broad yellow stripe painted up my back and custard flowing through my veins. I just muttered and moaned and emitted mysterious expletives at full volume. To describe this behaviour as undignified does it no justice at all. It was abject. I growled and grumped and took even greater offence when the opposition declared well before tea with a total only a whisker over 200. I now realise they were trying to make a game of it. We were in no state to respond to their challenge, but they weren't to know that. I felt we were being treated with a lack of respect, which was fair enough, as we were awful. I decided we would go for the draw from the off, and to help things along a little, I opened the batting myself.

History, happily, has not recorded the sheer ghastliness of the 9 I somehow amassed on that day, and my own memory has completely erased it. For once, though, the Rain Men showed notable powers of crease occupation. We batted for what seemed like days, with the style and brio of wallpaper paste. But you cannot resist for ever, especially against a much better team who were now beginning to feel a bit put out.

With 5.2 overs left, our ninth wicket fell.

All was lost.

Our last two batsmen were at the crease. They were the last tiny waggly tip of a shockingly long tail.

They were Terence, the Human Sieve; and Conrad, who, when counting his limbs, stops at three.

Neither of them was Mark Waugh either.

Indeed, Terence, although he has scored a few runs over the years, has always been vulnerable to the one bowled straight at his stumps. He has the defensive technique of a chest of drawers. Worse than that, sometimes, for at Leaden Roding once he leapt over a middle-stump yorker with a deafening squawk that rang out through the Essex countryside. In adjacent meadows it must have sounded as though someone had just done something unspeakable to a parrot.

Nor was Conrad the possessor of the world's soundest forward defensive. For the first time, I saw that his prosthesis might be a disadvantage. Suppose the ball pinged off straight into the hands of a close-in fielder. Would any umpire be able to resist lifting the finger? Oddly enough, there were one or two close-in fielders by this stage. Nine, as I remember it.

How Terence and Conrad survived those 5.2 overs I will never know. They were heroic. Towards the end they were even beginning to look assured. I believe it was each one's greatest achievement on a cricket pitch. (Only cricket fans would be able to understand and appreciate this.) And the draw was certainly the best result in Rain Men's history. To have brought a superior team down to your level: well, is there anything more satisfying in sport? We were exultant. We may not have had any killer instinct left, but we still had a small stock of buttock-clenching bloodymindedness. Our opposition, unfortunately, were less happy, especially with me. The following year they declined to play us. I can't say it came as a shock. The fixture secretary said it was because of the difference in ability between the teams. Very generously he didn't use the words 'It's because you personally are a twat' anywhere in the email.

The season ended eventually, thank God, with our annual tour of Penzance. ('How many matches do you play there?' asked my friend Russell. 'Just the one,' said I. 'So in what sense is it a "tour" as opposed to what would normally be called a "match"?' asked Russell.) In Penzance we play the Arts Club, who are as ramshackle a bunch of layabouts as you could hope to find in whites. In 2003 virtually none of their usual team could play, as they were all going to a funeral. Their replacements, the backbone of a local club side, beat us easily. It was the Arts Club's first ever victory, after fifteen years. 'What's up, Doc?' we all asked each other afterwards, munching carrots, as Yosemite Sam homed in for the kill.

12

L IS FOR LEADERSHIP

A captain is only as good as his team. This, to me, self-evident fact has been fiercely disputed by my team-mates, who have proposed an alternative formulation: a team are only as good as their captain. But I can't see that it's a captain's fault if his team can't take wickets, hold catches or score runs. It's a captain's burden, for sure, weighing him down rather as if Andy Moles and Arjuna Ranatunga had just jumped playfully on to his shoulders. And it's a captain's challenge – a problem he must try somehow to solve while maintaining his composure and dignity, and not stomping around the outfield like a two-year-old whose Smarties have been taken away.

But bloody hell, what provocation must we suffer? Players drop out at the last minute, wielding pitiful excuses. You email everyone directions to the ground, which they then forget to print out, so they must call you from their mobiles twenty minutes after the game has started, five miles away from where they are supposed to be. Then you discover that half the kit is in the car of someone who is not playing today, and is going on holiday tomorrow to South America, almost certainly to be kidnapped and imprisoned up-jungle for eight months while his relatives cobble together the ransom, and his car key is in his pocket, so there's no hope of getting hold of the kit until next season at the earliest. And all that is before you have gone in to bat and been out first ball.

I touched briefly on this subject ten years ago in *Rain Men*, for I felt strongly about it even then. 'Anyone can marshal the world's best cricketers into a series-winning fighting force,' I wrote. 'But I can't imagine that Michael Atherton has ever had to ring around all his friends on the first morning of a Test match because Graeme Hick has been told by his wife that he has to put up some shelves.' A decade later I wonder whether the course of English cricket would have been a mite smoother if Mrs Hick had issued this unreasonable command. But I still feel that, as many of our parents would say, a lot of Test players don't know they're born. For them, cricket teams only ever have eleven players in them. Michael Vaughan has never had to worry, on the morning of the match, about whether there will be enough Minty Kit Kats to go round at tea. Could he ever understand the simple glow of pleasure a useless batsman experiences when a blatant leg bye is given to him as a run because the umpire is so busy trying to remember the lbw law he forgets to signal it? Nor has Michael ever needed to ask himself what happens when so many batsmen have been bowled middle stump that you can't get the stump to stay in the ground any more.

I believe the village game has much to teach other sectors of cricketing activity. We are frequently criticised for not being tough enough, for playing only 'for fun', as though there is something wrong with that, and for not supplying enough players for the first class and international games. (An outrageous calumny. Robin and I are ready and available if selected, and would be happy to buy new boots for the occasion.) We are compared, always unfavourably, with Australian club cricket, where no one can play unless they are very good and under thirty-five. (This is the reason we have never contemplated a tour of that otherwise marvellous country. We have been told that there wouldn't be anyone to play us.)

But village cricketers, silent and modest though we may be (when asleep), represent a priceless source of cricketing wisdom. I myself have been playing the game for twenty-five years. Blimey. Where did the time go? (Probably where Neal's hair went, and Tim's temper, and one or two people's wives.) Twenty-five years. I think I deserve a medal, or at least a slow wide long-hop outside off-stump. After all, for most of those years I have been captaining an average-to-poor village side. I have faced defeat more often than the various captains of Bangladesh. I have, in all that time, failed to walk when out only once – when caught behind off the thinnest edge (which no one heard, but I felt) off the third ball of a nine-year-old boy *who had never bowled in a cricket match before.* I have played in rain, in snow, in freak hail-storms, at the Oval (once), on three continents (not out in two) and at Charlton-on-Otmoor more times than I can think about. With luck, in 2006, I will reach 1,000 career runs. What Hicky once achieved before the end of May will have taken me most of my adult life. I have been there and done that, neither of them particularly well. I thought about buying the t-shirt, decided not to, and regretted it forever afterwards. What, then, are the fruits of this long and ultimately pointless 'career'? A certain amount of acquired wisdom, I suppose, as well as a touch of arthritis in my knee. I must nearly qualify as an expert. Perhaps I could be the sort of slightly pompous expert who answers people's questions, occasionally scratching his chin thoughtfully to imply deep reserves of wisdom. Here goes then.

Dear Dr Berkmann,
First, the big ones. Heads or tails? Bat or bowl?
Name and address withheld

Dr B writes: Is it not bizarre that, as you walk out to the centre of the pitch with the opposition captain at the start of the match, so much of your brain should be concentrating on which side of the coin you should nominate? For years I fretted about this, until someone told me that heads comes up not 50 per cent of the time, as previously assumed, but 50.0000423 per cent of the time, owing to the greater wind resistance of the Queen's head. This turned out to be rubbish, but it gave me the excuse always to call heads, despite knowing that in August the greater heat and thinner air make tails come up approximately 100 per cent of the time. I still stick doggedly to heads, like the last child in the class to realise that they are the butt of a cruel joke.

As for the batting/bowling question, this has history. In Captain Scott, Harry, when captaining, would always insert the opposition. This was partly an aggressive, partly a defensive strategy. If he had the better bowlers and the pitch looked promising, he obviously wanted to have first use of it. And if the other team was palpably stronger, he wanted the chance to hold out for the draw batting second. Add the many occasions when the other team won the toss and chose to bat on a belter, and we seemed to spend whole seasons bowling first. This became a little dull. So rampagingly, deadeningly tedious, in fact, that we all decided when we started Rain Men that we would *always* bat first, however green the pitch, however overcast the sky. This may seem a little self-defeating. Indeed, it has proved completely self-defeating on several occasions, but only recently have players begun to question the policy. Finally, I think, we have got it out of our systems, and can now start choosing to bat or bowl first as conditions demand it. Assuming, of course, that we have the slightest idea of how to interpret those conditions, which is what Dermot Reeve would call 'a big ask'.

Some reasons to bat first: It's a beautiful day. The pitch looks flat. Our bowlers look fat. Three of our team are lost on the motorway. It looks like raining heavily, and chances

133

are we won't finish the game, and nearly everybody prefers batting to bowling if they are only going to do one of them. We are grievously outclassed, and want the game to be over as quickly as possible. We are sick of bowling first.

Some reasons to bowl first: It's cold and wet and the pitch hasn't been mowed so much as gently trimmed. Our bowlers are fit and raring to go. Steve Harmison has wandered up and asked if he can get a game. Half the team want to leave at six o'clock to go to parties and so would rather bat after tea and then drive off after they are out. We are grievously outclassed, but think we will be able to hang on for the draw. We are sick of batting first.

Dear Dr Berkmann,
Field placings. As a village captain myself I am always struggling to get people in the right places. Half of them don't go where they are put and the rest stonedrift blatantly between balls. What do you suggest?
Name and address withheld

Dr B writes: This is an unsolvable problem: experiments have shown that, asked to go to cover point, 47 per cent of fielders will go to extra cover, 32 per cent will go to backward point or gully, and 1 per cent will go to square leg. Many fielders regard it as your responsibility to remember where the field placings are, not theirs. As for stonedrift, I have come to the sad conclusion that there is no cure for it, other than death. Stonedrifters cannot stop themselves moving from the field placing to which they have been assigned; indeed, they are probably not even aware that they are doing it. And when a catch goes straight to where they should be, but anything between ten and eighty yards from where they have ended up, they look at you with a shrug as though it is your fault. You can always spot a captain on the field of play: if he is not shouting, he is the one with the vein pulsing dangerously in his temple.

Some bowlers like to set their own fields, which is fine, as everything that goes wrong afterwards is therefore their own fault. On occasion I have had to resist some of the more forceful requests of bowlers. Once, when asked if there was anything he wanted, Francis the sharp-toothed stockbroker replied, 'Yes, change the fucking wicketkeeper.' The Human Sieve hadn't missed that many, and I owed him money, so obviously I had to quell that little revolt. Other bowlers set 7–2 fields and then bowl everything down the leg side: they deserve everything they get, which includes being taken off after the second over.

Otherwise, though, I have a few rules of thumb that, so far, have helped me stave off that life-threatening cerebral haemorrhage. One, place the field so that as few people have to move between overs as possible. Mid–off becomes long leg and so on. We bowl our overs slowly enough as it is, so we have to find some way of speeding things up. And no one in the world walks more slowly than someone compelled to field at long-on both ends. Two, make your field roughly symmetrical, to ensure that only a bare minimum of fielders have to move when a left-handed batsman comes in. Identify which of your fielders have it within them to memorise four fielding positions – this is a rare talent, given only to a few – and entrust them to move around between balls and overs. Let everyone else take root, bud in the spring and bear fruit towards the end of August.

Three is, expect no one to field at short leg. Bowler will bowl slow long-hop, batsman will hit ball straight at short leg and you will henceforth only have ten fielders. Or nine if you only had ten before. Or eight if you only had nine before.

(But if twelve players have shown up, and one of them is sleeping with your wife, this could be the solution to all your problems.)

Four is, don't follow the ball: in other words, don't put a fielder where the ball has just gone. Following the ball is the classic signal of captainly weakness. The temptation can be overwhelming. Indeed it may actually be the sensible thing to put a fielder there. But by doing so you show everyone that you made a horrendous cock-up by not putting a fielder there earlier. Instead do it quietly at the end of the over, after the ball has been hit there another three or four times.

Five is, you can run but you can't hide, and your weakest fielders can't do either. If you are playing on a slope, put them uphill. Otherwise, first slip is always safe as no one is ever going to catch anything there. Square leg by the umpire isn't bad: there is always someone else running around behind to cut off the boundaries, and any catches taken there are instinctive, and therefore possible. And resist the bowler's desire to move a fielder who has just ballsed things up, because if you do, over half of all remaining balls in the match will go to that fielder and through that fielder's legs. Unlucky fielders are magnetic. But remember the most important rule: if in doubt, do a lot of shouting. It will distract everyone's attention, even if it doesn't solve anything.

Dear Dr Berkmann,
I think my captaincy is perfectly adequate, in some-times difficult circumstances. But I am constantly being criticised for it. Why can't people be more under-standing?
BCL, Trinidad

Dr B writes: Have you made the mistake of being the best player in a moderate team? As virtually all village teams are extremely moderate, everyone knows the perils of entrusting executive office to the highly skilled. For one thing they throw their weight around, scoring all those runs and taking all those wickets, catching everything and generally getting people's backs up. People don't turn up to cricket matches just to watch someone else do everything. They want the chance to fail, and they want it every week. Remember, in village cricket, when someone drops the first catch of the day everyone else on the field breathes a sigh of relief because it wasn't them. A captain has to understand such responses, and he is more likely to understand them if he feels them himself.

Most teams benefit by choosing a completely mediocre player as their captain. After all, what's so great about being captain? Whatever happens, it's just worry, worry, worry. Who to put in at number eleven who won't drive home in a huff? Who can score, or umpire, or field behind square on the leg side? Then the bowlers tell you they all want to bowl from the end without the sightscreen. It's a nightmare. How are you supposed to go out and concentrate on your own game with all that going on? So pass on the responsibility to someone who doesn't have a game of his own. Free yourself from worry. You know it makes sense.

Dear Dr Berkmann,
People think I'm eccentric because I always soak my Weetabix in gold-top milk for precisely forty-three minutes and fourteen seconds, and eat nothing but baked beans and golden syrup when I travel abroad. Would I be considered such a bare-faced loon in village cricket?
RCJ'R, address withheld

Dr B writes: Not at all. Village cricket is, some say, the final refuge for what mental-health professionals call 'distinctive behaviour'. My friend Maxie, who runs a team like mine, is well known for his unfortunate tendency to wail like a banshee whenever his younger brother is out for less than 50. His younger brother is the team's best batsman and tends to carry their hopes on his shoulders. But, whatever the circumstances, it can't be good for team morale to see your captain weeping publicly. And the opposition can only ever be encouraged by cries of 'Now we're *really* fucked!' ringing around the ground. Compared to this, your unusual dietary requirements and unconfirmed tendency to blindfold anyone you drive to your home seem to me very small beer. Have you thought of coming to play for us?

> *Dear Dr Berkmann,*
> I used to love captaincy, and I think I was pretty good at it. But with all the pressures of the job, I noticed that my own form began to suffer. What should I have done?
> *NH, Chelmsford*

Dr B writes: Well, as I said before, first thing you should do is hand over the captaincy to someone worse. Although, if the captaincy has made you worse, it's possible that there is no one worse than you to hand it over to. In which case, you're stuck with it, matey. Someone has to butter the sliced bread and put out the boundary flags while all his team-mates are in the pub before the game, and that someone is you.

As for the batting, there are several ways you can try and end a lean spell, not all of which involve threats to umpires.

As no one has the time or the inclination to practise properly during the season, you may not have held a bat between last week's embarrassing dismissal and approximately eight minutes before you have to bat this week, when you have just strapped on your pads and you ask, in a desultory fashion, whether anyone could bung a few balls at you. Someone will then bowl you an equally desultory leg-spin which you will fail to lay a bat on, thus not preparing you even slightly for the hostile fast bowling you are about to face in the middle. This 'practice' will therefore have made you less confident about batting than you were before, which is quite an achievement. So why do it? Here are some alternatives. 1. Very large drink of something. 2. Don't practise against a real bowler. Practise against an imaginary bowler. Play elegant drives and savage cuts without having to fetch the ball afterwards. Looks silly but so what? 3. Another large drink of something. 4. Nip behind the pavilion. Ring someone on your mobile and get them to call you back straight away. Take the call in full view. Gasp several times. Tell the rest of your team that your house is burning down. Run to car and drive away. No need to think about batting for another seven days.

Dear Dr Berkmann,
Were captains so much better in the past, as everyone always says? For various reasons I'd prefer to think that they weren't.
MPV, by email

Dr B writes: One of the masters of the captaincy art died in 2004. According to cricketing legend, Keith Miller tended to set his field by telling his players, 'Scatter'. On another occasion he omitted to nominate a twelfth man. Finding himself with twelve players on the field, he said, 'Well, one of you had better fuck off.' In four years as captain of New South Wales, his side won the Sheffield Shield three times.

> *Dear Dr Berkmann,*
> OK then, so tell me: what attributes does a modern cricket captain need?
> *MPV, by email*

Dr B writes: I asked my team-mates this in the pub after a game and we compiled a list. Cheerleader. Man-manager. Tactical mastermind. Warrior. Player of mind games. Psychotherapist. Head boy. School bully. Brilliant fielder (because if you drop a catch, it's incredibly hard to take off the bowler at the end of that over). Collector of match fees. Negotiator. Salesman. Opportunist. Sneak.

My team-mates told me I am without equal when it comes to collecting match fees.

Alternatively, consider what the 1952 MCC Coaching Manual has to say on the subject:

> Captaincy wins matches and can lose them but it should do more than that; it can make or mar a season, not only in terms of wins and losses but also in the

general satisfaction and happiness which playing cricket can bring . . .

A captain must be an optimist and inspire optimism in his side: he must show confidence in them in order that they may feel confidence in him. By personality and example he can set and keep his team alight . . .

Encouragement is everything . . . criticism should always be constructive: slackness and conceit alone merit and should get the rough side of the captain's tongue . . .

There's much to think about there, as I'm sure you'll agree. But I'll tell you one thing: I'm not giving anyone the rough side of my tongue.

13

RAINING ALL OVER THE WORLD

Running a team creates a momentum that, in hard times, enables you to carry on running the team. After our annus horribilissimus, as we sat around in Cliff's bar wondering whether the team could survive, I was already in the throes of arranging the 2004 fixtures. For some reason, most of the teams that had thrashed us were more than enthusiastic to have a chance of thrashing us again the following season. And of two or three new fixtures I had somehow chanced upon, one stood out: our first ever foreign tour under the Rain Men banner, to Sweden, to play Swedes.

Foreign tours are the ultimate cricketing self-indulgence. It's all very well driving around the country to play your favourite sport, but flying across the world beats it into a pulp. Fortunately Harry was very good at arranging these jaunts. As well as a medieval warlord he could have made an excellent travel agent. In the late 1980s and early 1990s we went to France three times, to Madrid, to Rome and, marginally more traumatically, for two weeks to Hong Kong and India. The monstrous consequences of this trip were outlined in gruesome detail in *Rain Men*. Let's just say that, after a fortnight of bickering, manoeuvring and all-round shoddy behaviour, one of our four games was cancelled because the other side simply didn't want to play us. One half of the team, in Hotel Cockroach, wasn't talk-ing to the other half of the team, who had decamped to Hotel Posh. At Delhi Airport, punches were thrown. One member of the party spoke darkly of legal action; a couple of others never played for the team again. And my then girlfriend, who had also come on the trip, dumped me a week after we returned, not that long after we had set the wedding date. More than a decade later, merely the thought of this tour makes me shiver. It was, as I remem-ber, the first time that Harry said, 'Never again'. But happily not the last.

And so, in January 1996, we found ourselves at Heathrow again, clutching cricket bags and smiling nervously. This time it was South Africa. Harry had been on holiday to Namibia the previous year and had bumped into a man who, rather foolishly, suggested we all come down and play a couple of games and stay at his gaff. He appeared to mean it, but even if he hadn't Harry would have taken him up on it. We had a week in Cape Town, with tickets for three days of the South Africa vs England Test match, and a week in Natal, at this man's up-country ranch. Three games had been fixed up, and there was the possibility of a fourth. Two-thirds of our party had been to Hong Kong and India, including Terence, Arvind and Francis. Everybody else we knew had refused to come. Harry had been compelled to place an ad in the *Sunday Telegraph* to fill the extra places. Four fine upstanding ringers from the Surrey leagues came forward, bearing impressive credentials. They were by far the most cheerful members of the group, but then they had never met any of us before.

Cape Town was invigorating, in a strange, alien kind of way. Never before or since have I seen so many huge, ruddy-faced white men with fingers like sausages eating so many huge steaks in so many restaurants accompanied by so many silent wren-boned women and bullying so many waiters of darker hue. When they were among their own kind in pubs and bars, the sausagey ones were by contrast strikingly, even formally polite. Such elaborate expressions of courtesy can't have been heard in the UK since the nineteenth century. Maybe it was to make up for the fact that no one ever smiled, even at babies. Charm appeared to have been banned by decree. Out-and-out merriment seemed too dangerous to risk.

The opposition's captain nodded to me matter-of-factly. I was slightly disappointed that he didn't click his heels. Our ringers all did exercises before going on to the field. The rest of us just smiled knowingly, and were unable to walk by sundown. A goodish side beat us by three wickets. I scored 0 not out off three enthralling balls.

Then we went to the Test. This was the bright new

dawn of Michael Atherton's captaincy, before the poor man had been ground down by endless defeat. On a baking hot day we sat on a slope that I understand has since been bull-dozed to make way for attractive seating, and drank vats of South Africa's favourite beverage, Castle Lite Beer (low in alcohol, high in burps). It's strange, having sat at home watching England cock it up on the TV for so many years, to travel halfway across the world and watch them cock it up only a few yards away. After four Tests the score was still 0–0. Atherton and Russell had saved the Durban Test with career-defining pluck, and Hansie Cronje, as far as we knew, had yet to embrace the Dark Side of the Force. On day two, as we lay on blankets with huge bubbles of carbon dioxide roaring through our digestive systems, a low-scoring match appeared to be drifting England's way. Fraser and Martin had been bowling their socks off, and the South Africans (whom all Australians implicitly believe to be chokers) had been giving their wickets away as though they were some sort of reward. Last man in was Paul Adams, on his debut. Amazingly small for a Test cricketer, and visibly nervous, he played and missed several times before somehow ferreting one down to backward point where Dominic Cork was lurking. By extraordinary coin-cidence this was where we were lurking too, holding our silly banners and praying quietly for an England victory. But Corky had other ideas. With his tongue wagging like a labrador's, he picked up the ball, turned round and threw it exactly halfway between the wicketkeeper and the bowler, a throw so wild and hopeless even mid-wicket couldn't retrieve it. Result: four overthrows, Adams off the mark, the stranglehold broken. Adams and David Richardson then added 70 for the last wicket and South Africa won in three days.

Our second game in Cape Town never materialised, and we relocated to Natal, where it was raining. Indeed, it had been the wettest summer for forty years. Could it have been otherwise? We settled comfortably into our host's guest ranch, which had a tennis court, a swimming pool and an enormous fridge for tinnies in the shape of a huge tinny (I still dream of it sometimes today). Although Harry had repeatedly assured our host that we weren't any good, our opposition for both matches was to include Robert Rollins and Darren Cousins, both then of Essex. In the first fixture at the scenic Pietermaritzburg Oval, Mr Rollins, who was having a few problems believing his eyes, bowled humorous leg-spin, and dismissed most of our best batsmen. Harry stayed there, however, compiling a gritty but far-from-gainly 42 that somehow made us look even worse than we were. We lost by three wickets. I made 5 not out.

The weather, though, remained a problem. Rain fell with unseasonal vigour. It was a bit like being on holiday in Ireland, only with snakes. By the middle of the second week even the tinny fridge could not prevent tempers fraying. Two of the ringers decided they hated each other. One of the Scott regulars, an actor and voice-over artiste of legendary sensitivity, demanded to be moved to a separate building to avoid having to hear the lavatory being flushed at night. Arvind started placing calls to India at three o'clock in the morning, which woke everyone up who hadn't already been woken up by the lavatory flushing. An impromptu tennis tournament became viciously hard fought, albeit with an ever decreasing number of balls. Every time anyone hit one over the fence into the uncultivated brush beyond, we considered it lost for ever as there were rumoured to be killer snakes out there. Eventually some employees of our host ventured out into the unknown to collect them up. They may still be laughing about this today.

Our final match was played under floodlights at a country club outside Pietermaritzburg. The Essex contingent, who may have seen us bickering on the tennis courts, suddenly sustained acute muscle strains and declined to play. Instead the opposition were captained by Paul Atkins, once of Surrey. We, in our satirical English way, were wearing dark blue jim-jams with our surnames picked out on the back in bright yellow. Playing under lights was a fascinating experience – a little like playing darts blindfolded, I imagine – and it might even have been fun as well, had it not been bucketing down with rain. I myself, as captain, was quite happy to call the whole thing off and repair to the bar, but our hosts said no, you've come all this way, we insist. Harry and the voice-over artiste opened the batting and soon ended up at the same end. Harry departed with the observation, audible in Botswana, that his partner was 'a selfish cunt'. As he wrote later in one of his match reports, the game 'went ahead in strained silence'. The ball was so slippery when we fielded that one of our ringers broke his cheekbone dropping a skyer. The other ringer who hated him was delighted. We lost by three wickets. I didn't get a bat.

Played three, lost three. In the event our ringers contributed 14 runs and six wickets between them, which endeared them to us all. As we left Harry was presented with an aggregate phone bill of £300, and Arvind insisted he had made no phone calls at all. This was brave, as Harry had bought an Assegai spear at some Zulu tourist trap. Arguments ensued. Between flights in a café at Charles de Gaulle airport Harry said both (i) 'Never again' and (ii) 'That little fucker will never play for Captain Scott if I have anything to do with it.' But Arvind is a useful player, and Harry loves to win games. He held out until the fifth game of the season before asking him back.

It was my last Captain Scott tour. (So far. As I keep telling Harry, never say never again.) Two years later they were off to Malaysia for ten days. Three Malaysian–Irish brothers had started playing for the team, and they had contacts. Harry told me later that it was much the happiest tour the team had undertaken, which may be why it has never interested me much. Only he of the entire party had ever been on a Scott tour before. The rest of them obviously didn't know what was required. There were no fights or savage arguments; no one stomped off in a fury and moved into a different hotel at any stage. So what was the point of that then?

The only potential problem was the length of the tour.

The Malaysian–Irish brothers had fixed it at ten days, but Harry could only get a week off work. He had to return three days early, which meant missing the last game. By this stage Harry had played 521 Scott games out of 521. A fine, possibly unique record was about to be tarnished. On the day of the Harryless game, everyone changed into whites. The fielders ambled out. The captain assigned them their positions. The batsmen walked out twirling their arms and adjusting their boxes, followed by the umpires. Just as the umpire at the bowler's end put the bails on the stumps, a light rain began to fall. Shall we start, he thought, or shall we wait until it blows over? He consulted the other umpire. The rain was becoming fiercer, but the forecast was favourable. So they retreated to the pavilion, the rain never stopped and the game never started. Had the rain held off for another ten seconds, and the umpire managed to say the word 'Play', Harry's record would have gone. Five years on, it is still intact.

'It was a great tour,' said Harry when I next saw him.

'Never again?'

'Never again.'

But in 2002 he came up with his best idea yet. A twenty-four-day world tour in which they would play just five games of cricket, *each on a different continent*. First they would fly to Bridgetown in Barbados for game one (thirteen hours in the air), then move on to Buenos Aires for game two (fourteen hours), fly to Sydney (nineteen hours) for the Test match, then to Perth (five hours) for their first ever defeat on

Australian soil, then to Singapore (five hours) to tick off Asia, finally to Cape Town (eighteen hours) to renew old acquaintances, and back home (twelve hours) having lost the kit, several credit cards and two team-mates, but all laden down with touristy tat they vaguely wished they hadn't bought. Didn't some of the flight times seem a little stretched? I asked. Ah yes, said Harry, but that's because they're not all direct flights. Bridgetown to Puerto Rico, Puerto Rico to Miami, Miami to Buenos Aires. All to save money, and to generate amusing anecdotes about deep-vein thrombosis.

They were due to leave on Boxing Day. Harry spent months putting the team together. It must have been a full-time job, dealing with travel agents and hotels and airlines, coercing his players to hand over thousands of pounds, and underwriting the whole venture himself when they delayed paying. He actually had twelve people signed up at one point. Then one of them, a journalist, was offered lots of money to do something else. Down to eleven. Then, a week before departure, his opening batsman rang up to say that his wife had told him he couldn't go. Fine, said Harry, but you should be aware that I am now going to sue you and your wife for the cost of the whole trip. His wife said he could go after all. Then another player, a South African, found out that he hadn't had his passport stamped when he had entered the UK and so, inadvertently, was an illegal immigrant. This emerged when the Australian High Commission refused his visa request and banned him from entering their country *sine die.* When I last saw Harry he was on the phone shouting at someone.

I must say I was tempted. Had I had the money or the time, and had Polly and I not had two children under four, I'd have volunteered. To be out for 0 on every continent: who of us has the chance to do that, other than Mark Butcher? But reality bit. I stayed at home. I have slightly regretted it ever since.

The itinerary looked gruelling on paper. In the flesh, like many England teams, it was worse than anyone had expected. In Miami, en route to Barbados, all the South Africans in the party were arrested because the airline had given them green forms on the flight instead of blue forms. Immigration refused to discuss their case until after their next flight was due to take off. Fortunately the flight was delayed by four hours and they managed to catch it, but not before fingers had been chewed down to stumps. After Barbados the team again flew to Miami en route to Buenos Aires. The South Africans were arrested again. It was on this stopover that one of the Malaysian–Irish brothers lost his beloved guitar. It shattered into bits as he tried to keep out a well-directed yorker.

With their unashamedly cosmopolitan selection policy the Scotts are not a bad team these days. Even so, we are only talking about a goodish village side, so Harry had emailed ahead, warning their opposition of five continents that, though enthusiastic, the standard of cricket they had to offer was not high. These emails were universally ignored.

In Barbados they faced a team that had not lost for two years. The Scotts made 150, which seemed OK, until they discovered during lunch that a competitive score on that pitch was 400. In Buenos Aires they faced an Argentina XI that included six members of the side that had recently beaten Holland in the ICC Trophy. Three of the other five were overseas professionals working as coaches. Scotts played their hearts out and lost by only nine runs. But by now exhaustion was setting in. So frequently were the Scotts flying that, according to their body clocks, they were playing every game in the middle of the night. British Airways had told Harry that there were no direct flights from Buenos Aires to Sydney, so they had to stop over at Auckland at 3.30 in the morning. But why wasn't anyone else getting off the plane? Because they were all going on to Sydney, of course. Couldn't the Scotts upgrade their tickets? Only at the British Airways desk at Auckland airport. This opened at 5 a.m. The plane took off at 4.50 a.m. without them.

They lost four of their five matches, as you'd expect, but three of them were by 9, 7, and 9 runs. In Singapore they played the Ceylon Sports Club, local cocks of the walk, and won a nailbiter by two wickets. Along the way there were only a few significant casualties. One middle-order batsman had told everyone to bring fancy dress for New Year's Eve. No one else did, and he managed to lose his Father Christmas outfit on the streets of Buenos Aires. Of the eleven players who went, only one was declared *persona non grata* by the other ten and banned from ever playing for the team again. 'That's not a bad ratio,' I told Harry over lunch after he had told me all the stories you have just read. But he was looking thoughtful. Antarctica may be their next destination, or possibly Mars.

14

INBOX

From: Simon
To: Marcus
Date: Sunday, February 29, 2004, 11:25 am

John and I did nets at the Oval Thursday. Went brilliantly. THIS is definitely going to be the year. We're going to keep going at least once a fortnight.

From: Simon
To: Marcus
Date: Thursday, March 11, 2004, 12:28 pm
Subject: Re: Rain Men 2004

How you have gladdened my heart. The fixture list is all wonderful news, except it doesn't start soon enough. Every time I make a cup of tea now I nip outside, spending the brewing time throwing a ball at an angled trampoline. Occasionally I even catch it.

You will of course be at least one chapter light in *Zimmer Men* when it turns out that all that practice I've done has paid off and my average soars. Then you'll have to find somebody else to be the butt of your jokes. Not that you'll have to look very hard.

You will be glad to hear that I believe I can make almost EVERY match. We are away first two weeks in August in Derbyshire so those two might depend on where the Weekenders and Godfrey Evans CC matches are being played. And, although in Yorkshire first week in June, we're coming back on the Saturday so Jane has said she can drop me off in Toddington. If you could arrange the 3/4 July match for the Sunday, that would be brilliant from my point of view.

Oh, and do you have the name of that online cricket equipment site you say is so good? Ta.

From: Simon
To: Marcus
Date: Thursday, March 11, 2004, 12:35 pm

Incidentally, finally found a 'how to' cricket DVD yesterday, the only one that seems to exist. Sketchy though my knowledge of cricket history is, though, even I realise that Don Bradman was playing cricket an awfully long time ago, so I thought it best to pass. Thought I might get the MCC Masterclass one. Is it any good, do you know?

Let me know your availability and keenness for cricket nets on Fridays. That looks to be a regular for us now. If we could get two hours, it makes sense to have three people. If you and someone else (Robin perhaps) were keen, we could try to book for two nets and alternate the coach.

At tomorrow's net things will certainly go to pieces. I was fairly euphoric at my progress last time but feel I ought to point out to the coach that if the ball comes to the leg side, I have a tendency to run backwards towards square leg!

From: Simon
To: Marcus
Date: Monday, March 22, 2004, 4:16 pm
Subject: Cricket, what else

Having trouble finding any way of getting a net and a lesson this week. But I've asked if there's time on Friday 2 April. If you could let me know a.s.a.p. if you can do this, that would be great.

It struck me, thinking about how GCSEs and 'A' levels

as well as top-level cricket have changed, that there's something intrinsically wrong with the game as we play it. It needs to be updated.

At school now, exams are no longer the be-all-and-end-all. A significant proportion of the eventual mark comes from doing coursework. Can't this be applied to cricket? If you've been doing very well in nets you should be able to somehow get a better mark than someone who simply turns up for the game and whacks the ball about. Not quite sure how this would work in practice (not at all I suspect) but isn't there some body I can propose it to?

From: Simon
To: Marcus
Date: Friday, April 30, 2004, 1:12 am
Subject: A thought too far

I realised tonight that Jane may be right about me having become obsessed.

Went to see a film – dreadful as it turned out. But it was a Universal movie and, as the Universal name came from around the globe, a terrible thought came into my mind. It suddenly occurred to me that if it had been a backlift, it would have been too far outside off-stump. This is no longer funny. I think I'm now finding cricket more interesting than women. Spring has been entirely spoilt.

From: Marcus
To: Simon
Date: Friday, April 30, 2004, 9:32 am
Subject: Re: A thought too far

I know what you mean. I have a particular pair of shoes that remind me of Alec Stewart. I have a teapot that conjures up the shape of Mark Butcher's head. Sadly I broke the sugar bowl that reminded me of Andrew Caddick's ears. Probably just as well.

Sometimes I look at Terence's bald dome and wonder whether it would take spin.

Still, at least you have finally realised that cricket is more interesting than women. After all, sex is over and done with in a few moments, unless you're Sting. Whereas a perfectly timed off-drive for four lives on in your mind for ever.

From: Simon
To: Marcus
Cc: Howard, Robin, Neal, Richard, Terence, Cliff, AJ and twenty-four others
Date: Wednesday, May 5, 2004, 3:50 pm
Subject: Weather forecast

Only ten days till the first fixture, but will it be rained off?

weather.co.uk only does nine days ahead. The forecast for Aylesbury on Friday 14 May is a high of 60, partly cloudy, with wind from the north at 14 mph. Every day bar next Thursday and Friday has rain clouds in it.

Anyone have a better forecast from anywhere else?

15

ACUTE/CHRONIC

The weather gods are not mocked. One spring I was in Cliff's bar with my friend Michèle, expressing trenchant opinions on the issues of the day with customary bar-room levels of intelligence and insight, when Michèle suddenly announced, possibly to keep herself awake, that it was going to be a scorcher this summer. I paused in my monologue.

'Possible heatwave,' she said.

Cliff and I caught each other's eye. Go no further, the eyes said.

'Four months of glorious sunshine,' said Michèle.

Stop right there. Do not tempt fate in this wilful and frivolous manner. But Michèle was on a roll.

'It could be the best summer in living memory,' she finished with a flourish.

Cliff and I groaned. We have been playing cricket for a long time. We know the weather gods, and we know that one idle comment in a bar on a Monday evening in March can change everything.

The following afternoon I was walking in the park with my first-born, enjoying some unseasonal spring sunshine. Then, from nowhere, dark clouds appeared. Furious rumbles of thunder were heard. Raindrops the size of Mike Gatting began to fall. The infant and I were at least an all-run four from the nearest shelter. Twenty seconds later we were drowning in the mud of Passchendaele. Even the Brumbrella couldn't have saved us. The weather gods were showing us who's boss.

It was therefore supremely pointless of Simon to speculate on how the weather would turn out in ten days' time. Chaos theory teaches us that tiny events can have vast ramifications, that the flutter of a butterfly's wing in Taiwan can eventually cause a hurricane at Sabina Park, should the weather gods desire it. The uncountable profusion of these tiny events means that it is mathematically impossible to predict the weather with any degree of certainty more than four, or at a pinch five, days in advance. But that doesn't stop us looking it all up on websites ten days beforehand. Indeed, nothing could stop us, short of worldwide computer meltdown. It's not idle curiosity. *We need to know.*

Each year the Rain Men start playing cricket later than most teams because we don't want to play in the wet and cold of April. I don't think this is unreasonable. For years the Captain Scott season kicked off at Englefield Green in

Surrey. I hear it is beautiful during the summer, but in April it was like playing on permafrost, with evil Antarctic squalls scything through your thermal long-johns and three sweaters as though they weren't there. There must have been a point on the ill-fated polar expedition when Scott, Oates, Wilson and Bowers thought to themselves: Are we absolutely sure this is a good idea? But at least they were allowed to wear gloves. Englefield Green had no such consolations. Watching Arvind bowl in an overcoat can't have been many people's idea of leisure time well spent. So when we started Rain Men I decided there would be No More Games in the Bleak Midwinter, Even If It Calls Itself Spring.

Every season since, of course, there has been a brief, glorious heatwave in late April and early May, succeeded by a freak relapse into winter three days before we start playing. There is no second-guessing the weather gods. Ditto the coin gods, who have big teeth and nasty little horns, and laugh out loud whenever I call 'heads'. And let's not even mention the lbw gods, who, according to the ancient texts, have index fingers even longer and knobblier than Steve Bucknor's.

This is the second time we have played Molins/ Westbourne, a works team with a well-tended ground near High Wycombe. Both times it has been the first game of the season. Last year I could only raise a team of eight, which is another reason for starting as late as possible. Enthusiasm for the forthcoming cricket season cannot be taken for granted. True, some of us have been thinking about this moment since September, but for Tim and Bill and one or two others (as well as all newspapers) May is still the football season. Like ocean liners, they need time to adjust. Only playing some cricket will fire up their enthusiasm for cricket. Some Rain Men don't want to play at all until they have played at least three times. And one or two, like Richard, are perpetually searching the heavens for a strange orange ball of light that is widely reputed to shine during the summer months. When they see it, but not before, they sign up for some games. Consequently, the first game of the season is always hard work. Finding a team. Then finding the kit. Then getting someone to smell the kit. And then we turn up and realise that we have completely forgotten how to play this stupid game. Perhaps having a couple of nets – or in Simon's case, thirty-seven – might have helped after all.

Still, there are certain aspects of the first game of the season that never change. The comforting squeak of new pads. The joyous rip of old cricket trousers. Overall, the feeling of strangeness, for I think this is the only time in the year you realise this is quite an odd thing to do. Pity the professionals who play all year round, for they do not get to rediscover cricket every April or May as the rest of us do. Many of our fielders, even the reliable ones, cannot remember whether they catch the ball with hands up or hands down. Captaincy, in particular, is a voyage of discovery, and I am slightly more shrill and desperate in my commands than I will be in July. But one or two things haven't changed. I lose the toss, and my opening bowlers don't take any wickets.

Winter has eroded our memories of last season. Just as mothers are biologically programmed to forget the pain and trauma of having a baby so that sooner rather than later they will contemplate having another one, so cricketers are programmed to forget the pain and trauma of losing by nine or ten wickets every week, or hundreds of runs. Halfway through her second labour, Polly suddenly remembered everything. 'Fuck!' she said, or rather screamed at the top of her voice. This is just how I feel when Martin, our former fast bowler, concedes 32 off three overs and has to be taken off (according to Richard, approximately three overs too late).

There are many moments of acute misery in cricket. Getting out, dropping a catch, conceding 32 off three overs: they all feel like tiny stab wounds to the heart, or some other part of the body you have injured but which hasn't properly healed up yet. When we look back at a match, we tend to remember the tiny stab wounds and forget most of the rest. It's as though each match is made up of a few small but memorable disasters separated by long periods of nothing very much happening. But when you are out there fielding, and nothing very much is happening, and your opening bowlers are clearly never going to take a wicket, even if they snorted a bagful of cocaine and painted the ball green, you realise there is another sort of misery in cricket, a quieter, more chronic misery. You can be bowling and fielding, ball after ball, over after over, and you realise you have absolutely no idea where the next wicket is coming from. Every ball hits the middle of the bat. Your bowlers are trying to create a little pressure in the minds of the batsmen, and failing. Perhaps the wicket is too good. More likely, the bowling is not good enough. Eventually you start waiting for the batsman to make a stupid mistake. You have given up trying to earn a wicket. Now you are praying they will give it to you as a present instead. At the start of the game you were playing poker, although you knew your hand wasn't strong. Now all you are left with is a lottery ticket, and the one chance in fourteen million that your number will come up.

This, I think, is where the best Test cricketers really earn their crust. Most of us in these circumstances would give up completely, and indeed as a viewer I often give up completely and go and do something more interesting instead. It's too painful to watch Australia scoring 500 off us yet again, when you could be digging the garden, or leaping off Canary Wharf to your death. Test players, though, must keep going, for that is their job. Indeed, how they deal with failure often tells us more about them than how they deal with success. (It has told us a lot about England cricketers for more than thirty years.) When I am not captaining, I try and shut off from everything, to still my emotions and become the zen cricketer. Concentrate on the next ball. Don't you worry 'bout a thing. It doesn't matter, it isn't my problem. And yet, somehow, my shoulders always manage to slump of their own accord. My mind is positive, but my body language radiates lack of hope.

Because it's contagious. Today, all around the field, shoulders are between three and five inches lower than at the start of play. Spirits are several inches lower than that. As captain, I am standing at first slip, trying to look as though I know exactly what I am going to do next. This takes up all the mental energy that would otherwise be used in trying to work out what to do next. It's not surprising, under such intense pressure, that the mind begins to wander.

Look at that cloud. It looks exactly like . . . a hawk. No, a sheep.

A police siren. Coming towards us, coming towards us, going away from us, going away from us . . .

Oh, look, there's a train on that bridge.

Was that a catch that just flew past my right shoulder?

Yes, it's definitely a sheep, that cloud. The one next to it looks like that TV chef with the beard . . .

The minutes stretch into hours, or possibly months. I now have gloomy Bill bowling at one end, who last season took four wickets at 42, and Andrew-with-the-ponytail at the other, who took two at 43.5 . . .

The weather gods are not mocked. It is now glorious sunshine.

Two consecutive maidens. I hold my breath. Both these bowlers are finding some control, from somewhere.

Shoulders start to unslump. Everyone is paying attention now.

And then the batsman misses one and is bowled. It is our first wicket of the season, after a mere forty-two minutes' play. We are exultant. None of us can believe it. The taller players exchange high fives, while the shorter ones slap backs and shake hands. (There is nothing in sport less dignified than trying to reach a tall person's high fives and failing.)

Martin's opening spell might have implied otherwise, but it turns out to be quite difficult to bat on this wicket. We dismiss Molins for 180, a total boosted by a wild swiping 44 from their number eight. Bill takes three for 34, Andrew-with-the-ponytail three for 37. It is nearly a whole season since we bowled out the other side, so, although we are then all out for 82 (Berkmann 0 not out) and lose by 98 runs, we leave encouraged. We have been crushed by the wheels of industry, but we are still smiling. Either we are feeling strangely optimistic about the games to come, or we are congenital idiots. And if the latter, at least we are congenital idiots who have been mugging up on their field positions.

From: Simon
To: Marcus
Date: Sunday, May 16, 2004, 10:42 pm
Subject: All Becomes Clear

Just remembered that, as I was fielding at extra cover, I saw a solitary blackbird on the opposite boundary (where a deep backward square leg might be).

As far as I'm concerned, that explains my duck yesterday.

16

YOUNG

One of the more vivid impressions I had of that Molins/ Westbourne game – during the brief periods I was sufficiently alert to have any impressions at all – was how young they all were. Where had they found them all, these lithe young specimens, with their unlined faces and slightly self-absorbed expressions? Youth, of course, is wasted on the young, who haven't the slightest idea that one day soon they will no longer be bright-eyed and bushy-tailed. The Rain Men, rheumy of eye and scraggly of tail, look on in envy. We have learned a lot over the years, and one of the most significant things we have learned is that blissful ignorance has much to be said for it. How lucky they are to know so little. How annoying they are for appearing to know how lucky they are. And how annoying they are generally, with their bad driving, their stupid hair, their ridiculous opinions and their catastrophic taste in clothes and music. More infuriating yet is that young women seem to fancy them rotten, valuing youthful vitality over . . . well . . . whatever it is we have to offer. There's no justice.

Nevertheless, like many ageing sides, we feel obscurely that we too could do with some young people on the team, to pep us up and do all that running-around stuff we find so awkward nowadays. Not surprisingly we want the team to survive, not just till next season, but for ever. Men father children to preserve their genes; in this case our cricketing genes are at stake. I heard myself saying recently that if Rain Men are still going in twenty years I will feel I have done my job. But why? It doesn't actually matter in any great scheme of things. It just matters to me and my friends. It feeds our egos to think that the team will go on without us. For our egos are hungry. Absolutely ravenous, in fact. They have consumed a huge lunch but are already thinking of tea, and a big dinner later, and maybe a late-night snack when they get home.

So yes, we would like to recruit some young people, especially if they can play a bit. But where are they? We have looked, in a desultory sort of way, but found none. Admittedly we have no ready supply of teenagers ourselves, as most of our kids are too young. And there is a limit to the amount of interest you can express in other people's teenage sons, for fear of being outed as some sort of Uncle Monty-like perv. We are not the only team in this situation. Other teams too are failing to recruit from the fountain of youth. Many young people, it turns out, simply don't like cricket. They regard it as an old person's game. They would rather play football. Of course they would. Football is more cool than cricket. ('Cool', I acknowledge, is now an uncool word for the concept of cool, but as the cool word for cool changes almost daily, and would certainly be uncool by the time you read this, I shall use the word 'cool' to mean cool in its coolest sense. However uncool it may be to do so.)

Cricket has an image problem. We know this. Young Afro-Caribbeans are no longer drawn to the game, to the despair of their cricket-mad elders. In some previously hard-fought leagues, old crocks are keeping their places in teams because young players are not coming through to replace them. And while we know that cricket is constantly adapting to survive, non-fans seem to believe that the game has scarcely changed since the end of the nineteenth century, that many top players wear enormous beards and top hats and employ manservants to polish their boots. It's absurd. We now know that David Gower only employed one manservant to polish his boots, and was occasionally known to put them on himself. To suggest otherwise is to tarnish the reputation of a great national servant.

Cricket's fuddy-duddy image will always be hard to eradicate, though, while Tests are being played at Lord's. Most cameras concentrate on the play out in the middle, but there always seems to be one mischievously trained on the pavilion and the dribbling wrecks who sit outside, impatiently waiting for the next meal. No one there is under fifty-five. If you were just fifty-eight they would probably call you a 'new bug'. Required to wear jackets and those admittedly rather pleasing ties when the ambient temperature at the ground is equivalent to Gas Mark 4, these ancients doze peacefully, even though Flintoff has just scored 50 in thirty-five balls. Many of them are wearing Old Man's Trousers, where the position of the belt is completely random, their waists having been obliterated by decades of not-quite-fully digested steak-and-kidney puds. Four are actually dead, and one has been sitting there since March. In no sense do they qualify as 'a pretty sight'.

And they confirm everyone's prejudices. To the young they say that cricket is a gerontocracy. To the wider cricket-ing world they say that the sport in this country is still run by Sir Gubby Allen from beyond the grave. That although the British Empire effectively ceased to exist half a century ago, English cricket is its last outpost. English cricket, mean-while, seems only too happy to promote this idea. I think instantly of the Hon. Tim Lamb, who until 2004 was Chief Executive of the England & Wales Cricket Board. When he bowled medium pace for Northants in the 1980s, the Hon. was a perfectly ordinary-looking person with normal hair. Then he retired and entered Lord's. When he re-emerged a few years later, he had become a fully formed administrator. His hair was grey and slicked back with greasy stuff, and he only ever wore a blue blazer with gleaming golden buttons. This may indeed be the required uniform for a CEO of the ECB. But by my reckoning the Hon. was only in his mid-forties when he started looking like this. I know no one in his mid-forties who looks like this. True, one or two may dress like this in the privacy of their own homes, when their wives are away and they know no one is going to call, but I doubt any of them would have the courage to pop down to the newsagents in such apparel. The message to the world, however, is clear. English cricket is run not by old men, but by youngish men who have voluntarily transformed themselves into old men before their time. No wonder the Hon. became so hard to take seriously.

To gain power, therefore, you must seek the approval of a small constituency of furious youth-hating elders. And to promote the game, which is your job, you have to appeal to everybody else, particularly those missing young people who don't know what they are missing. Hence the recent attempts by the ECB and others to rebrand English cricket as 'cool'.

You know what I am talking about. Tom Jones impersonators and Atomic Kitten playing between innings at one-day internationals. Calendars with photos of England players trying to look like Clint Eastwood in *A Fistful of Dollars*. Official encouragement of James Anderson's hairstyles.

The administrators know that young fans need to be encouraged, if only to replace the older ones who are steadily popping off. At county matches the spectators are now so ancient that no one bothers calling an ambulance when one of them keels over and dies: there's already one standing by to cart off the corpses. Derbyshire famously let slip a few years ago that their membership, already perilously low, included sixteen dogs. But how many of those dogs were still alive? And how many were still alive but unable to attend matches regularly because their owners had died of old age?

Nonetheless, I'm not sure that attempts to be cool are the answer. Indeed, the cooler cricket tries to be, the more it resembles your fat uncle dancing at a wedding. Atomic Kitten are a case in point. Who were they supposed to appeal to, exactly? The blazers had obviously heard of them from somewhere. Perhaps they had sent a young person round to Woolworths to see who was number one in the hit parade this week. They probably thought that hiring a trio of comely young women to sing their useless covers of Kool and the Gang hits on a stage at deep third man would gain them some bit of publicity. In this they were right. Newspapers queued up to laugh at them. But pop music is a fragmented business these days. Atomic Kitten, less a musical unit than a marketing concept, were exclusively aimed at and bought by girls aged between eight and thirteen. (I say 'were' because they have since split up.) How many girls between eight and thirteen go to one-day internationals? And how many of the cricket fans listening to Atomic Kitten that day thought, 'Oh! What a good idea! I've wanted to see Atomic Kitten live for ages! I have all their hits!' Only the Hon. Tim Lamb, I would guess. And even he was really thinking of the Beverley Sisters.

Grovelling to young people is never worth the effort. Either you get it wrong and look stupid, or you get it right and wonder why you bothered. Cricket will never be cool; I write that with a wonderful feeling of relief. The most popular player of the day is Andrew Flintoff, and he wouldn't know how to be cool if he tried. People talk of Flintoff as the village cricketer writ large, and there is an element of truth in that. Village cricketer, in that he plays for the fun of it and likes a drink and a curry afterwards. And writ large, in the sense that he is built like a buffalo. Village cricketers, of course, know there's no point trying to be cool. The day you stride out to the crease full of your own marvellousness is the day you hit the ball straight up into the air, a bird shits on your cap and your trousers fall down. We know better than to tempt the fates in this way, or indeed in any other way.

Still, we need those young people. One team we know has been struggling with this problem for years. The Imploders, as we shall call them, have aged together, and many players have retired, ostensibly to encourage the next generation. Except that the next generation can't or won't take up the responsibilities offered. Slackjawed with cider and/or crack cocaine, they can't be bothered to captain, look after the pitch or sometimes even turn up to play. The four remaining oldsters continue to run the team and are constantly beset by Jasons and Lees dropping out en masse the night before the game, which therefore has to be cancelled. When the Imploders do manage to cobble a team together, the Jasons show signs of talent but give the game away time and again. The resultant string of crushing defeats erodes their enthusiasm yet further. Only their regular victories over legendary incompetents the Main Ren (anag.) keep them going at all.

At this point it would be all too easy to emulate F.S. Trueman and shake your head in mute disgust at the shocking lowering of standards everywhere. You know that you have hit forty when you start to regard all young people as feckless and moronic, forgetting that you were that way yourself about half an hour ago. Young people need encouragement, as well as National Service and bromide in their tea, which none of them drink anyway as it's no longer cool. (Nor, apparently, is it hot.) We can bring these errant striplings into the fold. It may take a little lateral thinking, that's all. Here are a few ways we might do it:

• Sledging. Many young people feel that cricket is too gentlemanly a game for their more rugged temperaments. Put them right. Tell them about Steve Waugh. Show them videotape of Glenn McGrath mouthing 'You fucker' after every ball. Sledge them yourself during breakfast. 'Call that a haircut you little bastard?' and so on. Few self-respecting young people can resist this for long.

• Replica kits. Is your teenager wearing an appalling replica football shirt that makes you want to vomit? Tell him how you feel. Say there is no clothing in the world more loathsome or repulsive. Say that on second thoughts there is. Say that the current England one-day international strip is marginally more emetic. Watch as he goes straight out and buys it.

• Girls. Football has long had the advantage here, for in the Premiership even the thickest central defender with a face like a potato seems to have his pick of the world's top models. And yet there are possibilities. In South Africa many top cricketers have hooked up with astoundingly pretty catwalk lovelies. Even Jacques Kallis, who once arrived on a tour of England with a middle parting in his hair, has managed to snare one. The only time I have ever seen him in the flesh close to, he was wandering forlornly around the boundary at Arundel like a lost wildebeest, and yet top Afrikaans model Minkie van der Heffalumpen, or whatever her name is, has fallen for his charms. So there's hope for us all, including your reluctant teenager.*

• If all else fails, bribery. Persuade your teenager or unemployed young person still living at home and leeching off you like a parasite to come and play cricket in return for tax-free payments of money or small consignments of drugs. They will be so amazed when you offer the latter that they might actually turn up. Then give them the customary small bag of self-raising flour (as seen on thousands of American cop shows after disastrous drug busts). Claim you were rooked by the local dealer. Only if your teenager turns out to be the local dealer can this plan go wrong.

* This is a lie.

17

INSULT/INJURY

Some incidents.

• At Brook in Surrey, where we rarely flourish, Gloomy Bill finds a strip to his liking and takes three wickets. Brook are wobbling, or at least shaking in the breeze, at 60 for four. A young Zimbabwean comes to the wicket. He looks useful, if agricultural. Third or fourth ball he goes for a huge welly on the legside and pops it up off the back of the bat to Bill, who is at that nameless position 45 degrees behind square leg on the single. (Deep leg gully? Short long leg? Not-particularly-fine fine leg?) It is the World's Easiest Catch, so of course Bill fluffs it. The ball has looped up towards him; he need not move an angstrom unit in any direction; he has just taken three wickets so is full of confidence; the sun is behind him; and this is the catch that, if taken, could give us the only chance of victory we will ever have on this ground. The Zimbabwean goes on to score 103 not out. During the carnage I throw the ball to Francis. He bowls tidily and removes the other batsman. First ball of his third over, the young Zimbabwean hits the ball fantastically hard, straight back at Francis. So hard, in fact, that Francis does not have time not to go for the catch. Even a tenth of a second more would have given him time to think again and remove his hand from the path of the ball. The ball hits the tip of the third finger of his right hand. Francis concedes 23 from this over, equalling the team record for profligacy, and asks to be taken off as his finger hurts. He will later establish that he has broken it not laterally, as most people break fingers, but longitudinally, from the tip down to the joint. He will wear a curious contraption that makes him look like Captain Hook for two months, and he will not play for the rest of the season. For this he will blame Bill. Indeed, every so often during the summer I will receive an email from him in which he slags off 'that useless fat bastard' for dropping the catch.

• Later in the same match Gloomy Bill pulls a muscle and drops down the order to eight. We have recovered from 19 for five to 64 for six, but defeat seems inevitable. Bill asks for a runner, and Sam the youth policy is chosen. Unable to watch, I go inside for a pee, and when I return Bill is on his way back, having been run out. Simon is in next. Marginally more self-absorbed than Sir Geoffrey Boycott, with a similar reputation for tactlessness, he tries to engage the outgoing batsman in conversation.

Simon: How's the wicket playing, Bill?
Bill: I've just been run out. Fuck off, Simon.

Everyone leaves the changing room to allow Bill to throw his bat around a bit and bang his head against the wall. Out at the wicket, Simon attempts to engage the other batsman in conversation. This is John, his regular netting compadre, who went to school with Kim Hughes. It is well known that John does not like chatting at the wicket, as he says it disturbs his concentration.

Simon: So what happened there? Whose fault was it?
John: Fuck off, Simon.

Simon has what one seasoned observer will later call 'a hissy fit' and is out for 1. I wander round to the other side of the pitch, lie on the grass, close my eyes.

• Several weeks later, in an otherwise amiable and well contested game, Tim the formerly incredibly angry fast bowler is bowling and the batsman edges a delivery fairly straightforwardly to the wicketkeeper. (I say 'fairly straightforwardly', but we will take only two other wicketkeeping catches all season.) Several of us leap in the air, but the batsman isn't walking and the umpire isn't fingering. Simon, who is fielding at mid-off, will later tell me he didn't hear it, which may explain the umpire's reaction but not the batsman's. Tim reacts with staggering equanimity. His newly grown midlife-crisis sideburns barely twitch. Perhaps he didn't hear the edge either. Whereas, at square leg, I feel a red mist coming on. 'That's a fucking outrage!' I shout. If I had been wrong and the batsman had been innocent, he would have reacted, but he doesn't. I am conscious of the need to rein in my temper in order not to lose another fixture. In the event Gloomy Bill takes six for 24, our best-ever figures, and we win the game by 9 runs. But I drop three catches, get a monstrous attack of cramp in my calf while dropping the third, sit in front of the pavilion and mutter dark words for the rest of the game and brood over the incident for about two weeks.

Walk, damn you. Walk.

• At Faringdon the following week, we are again in the game, mainly thanks to an impressive opening spell from our steadiest bowler, Gags. He has their best batsman tamed and a wicket feels imminent. Then, as he runs round to field the ball at extra cover, we hear a snap and Gags falls over in a humorous fashion. We all laugh, assuming that one of the children have thrown something at him and he's making a meal of it. But no, it was his calf muscle going ping. Gags limps off and we lose by 37 runs.

Much discussion later about the indignities of ageing. Generally agreed that Gags's arc through the air after his muscle went ping wouldn't have been half as funny if he had been twenty-four years old rather than forty-four. One player points out that when we are fielding, people are nipping off for a pee far more often now. It's bad enough having to go in the middle of the night, but in the middle of the over too? And when you can bear it no longer and sprint back to the pavilion, there's someone in the loo already with even worse prostate problems than you, tinkling away dismally.

Next thing we know, we'll be feeling the cold more, like those old people who wear overcoats on warm summer days.

• Simon has a go at wicketkeeping. The following day I email to ask him if he is all right. He reports 'twinges from circular weals on chest, upper arm, shoulder and inner thigh', and one of his fingers 'now has the colour, size and flexibility of a small aubergine'. He asks if he can do it again next week. He also expresses his belief that his cricket obsession has peaked. 'I've worked out that I have spent more at the Oval on lessons in the past two months than I have earned in the same time, which is ridiculous, particularly as it has done little good. Have vowed never to go there again. Just have to face up to the fact that I'm not very good, aim lower, and settle for that.'

• The following weekend Simon hits 12 not out. It is his first foray into double figures, in his forty-fifth game for the team. 'Is it true I did a cover drive on Saturday as Richard says? I can't remember any of it except trying to charge the bowler and falling over and trying to scramble back to the crease, in a way reminiscent of a Mack Sennett comedy (one of his lesser-known cricket shorts).' To eradicate this technical problem, he books some more coaching sessions at the Oval.

• On Tuesday 22 June, I am in Winchester, early for a meeting. I walk down the road, idly looking for a bookshop, staring up at the clouds and thinking, what a lovely day. Suddenly I trip on the kerb and fall very painfully. (Afterwards, everyone says 'You should sue Winchester City Council.' But the kerb was perfectly clearly marked with bright yellow paint. I just wasn't paying attention. It was entirely my fault.)

I am lying on the pavement. I look at my right foot. It's at about 45 degrees to the direction it should be pointing in.

My first thought is: Bugger.

My second thought is: My meeting's in twenty minutes. How am I going to get there?

My third thought is: I haven't had a proper bat this season.

It's true. I haven't. Because the pitches have been slow, I have been putting myself in at number ten or eleven. I hit a square cut for four in the game against Brook Strollers, but otherwise have barely faced a ball. There would always be later in the season, I figured. There always is.

Someone has called for an ambulance. I feel no pain, but I know I will. A dislocated ankle looks horrible, by the way. A small crowd has gathered and they think so too. I am slightly uncomfortable, so move my foot an inch or two and click! the bone pops back in. The ambulance arrives. I am now sitting on a nearby step as though nothing has happened. The ambulance men smile, check it's not broken, send me on my way. I realise later that they simply don't believe that I have dislocated my ankle, as what has happened is simply not possible.

Indeed, over the next few weeks, I will discover that not only is properly dislocating an ankle hard to do – motorcycle accidents are really your only hope – but it is also an extremely serious injury, involving broken bones, major surgery, general anaesthetic and, for a forty-three-year-old man in something less than the peak of physical condition, a painfully long recovery period. I will be seen by consultants rather than junior doctors because I have an 'interesting' injury. I will be told that I have unusually shaped feet – Polly has been saying this for some years and has often asked me whether there were any ducks in the family. The doctors will establish that I have dislocated not the ankle bone itself but another joint close by. I haven't broken a bone, merely damaged ligaments and tendons. Everyone says I have been incredibly lucky, particularly because the bone clicked back in after two or three minutes. I'll need crutches for a week or two. No sport for a month.

Should be fit for the Swedish tour, though.

• The following weekend. We are playing St Anne's All Stars in south London. I am not playing, obviously, but I am there, partly because we have someone new playing who knows no one else, partly because I have this book to write and need to take some notes, and not at all because I am a very sad man who cannot keep away. Yet again we are flourishing against a team who usually beat us easily. Simon opens the batting and scores 11, including his second ever 4. Cliff goes in at number three and is biffing the ball to every corner when Bill comes in to bat.

Bill: Do you want to know how many runs you've made?

Cliff: No.

Bill: 85.

Two balls later Cliff is bowled. He thought he was on about 70. His highest ever score is 86. The ground has no sightscreens and is surrounded by tall trees, so on the All Stars' suggestion we are playing with a white ball. In the pub afterwards Cliff will reveal for the first time in the sixteen years I have known him that he is colour-blind. He will say that he often struggles to see the red ball and that the white ball is much easier.

We score 196 for four in our thirty-five overs. This is unquestionably a winning score. As we start tea the rain begins. Soon it is bucketing down. Seagulls perch in the upper branches of a tree.

'Look, it's easing up already,' says Bill.

As lightning flashes we tramp off woefully to the pub, looking (and feeling) as though we have all just taken baths fully clothed.

• And so to the match that began this book, against Charlton-on-Otmoor on 11 July. They score 329 for one declared. As I hobble around the boundary, I think: Thank

God I don't have to captain this. While I'm out of action we are rotating the captaincy and it's Cliff's turn this week. Next time I ask him to captain he will say no, he never wants to do it again.

Their innings grinds on. I am pushing my two-year-old on the swing when Sam the youth policy ambles over. Trying to field one of big Phil's more violent caresses, he has hurt the little finger on his right hand. He suspects it is broken. (It is. He too has broken it longitudinally, and he too will have to wear the Claw of Death for the rest of the season. We are increasingly a team of cyborgs.) Richard comes off next. He tried to take a caught and bowled and now has a big bruise on the palm of his hand. To be this outclassed is no fun at all. There's no point playing against someone as good as Phil. When other teams import ringers I feel aggrieved because there is no need for it: they would probably win anyway, and renting a ringer just makes the whole day pointless. But none of this applies at Charlton because Phil is their captain. If it were any other team we would just drop the fixture. But, first with Scotts and now with Rain Men, I have been playing against Charlton for twenty-five years. We have history together. I have played against several generations of Coopers and Launchburys, and have known Richard Howard, their fixtures secretary, all my adult life. Phil was probably only about five when we started coming here. We can't not play Charlton. Although it will be interesting to see how easy it is to raise a team against them in twelve months' time. All these thoughts run through my mind as our openers walk out to bat.

A few balls later Neal walks back. 'That was quite the stupidest shot I've ever played'.

'Oh, are you out?' says Simon.

Neal gives him a look.

Sam sits disconsolately with his finger in a mug full of ice. He says it's stinging and burning. He looks thoughtful for a moment. 'Have you ever licked the inside of a fridge freezer?' No one answers. We are all busy wondering about Sam's home life.

Richard is out. Sam passes him the mug full of ice.

I am scoring. All the usual detritus litters the scorer's desk. One lost batting glove. The batsman's cigarettes. A jar of Arnica cream.

Me: Ah, Robin's on 9.

Neal: What's his highest score this season?

Me: Well, I think this is.

Neal: What, he hasn't made double figures?

Me: Don't think so.

Gags: Oh don't say that. He'll be out next ball. He hasn't made 10 all season. He'll be out next ball.

We turn to watch. Robin tries to pull a short ball. It keeps low and bowls him behind his legs. Several Rain Men wail like Klingons. The game is over and the pub beckons us, telepathically.

18

PARADISE

The doctors said a month, but I never had any illusions. The ankle is swollen and painful, and although I am now using only one crutch, and then only outdoors, I resemble a fit person as closely as I resemble Floella Benjamin. First the doctors, then the osteopath, have said I just have to be patient, which is doctor-speak for 'This will take much longer than you think.' As someone generously equipped with nervous energy, I have been used to bounding around the house like a slightly frantic goose. Now I am hobbling around the house, and even that hurts. I have been compelled to stop moving, to spend more time sitting or preferably lying down, with foot resting on a small hillock of cushions, as I bark out orders to my family for more tea and biscuits. In the newspaper, which I feel obliged to read from end to end, I learn of Mark Butcher's injury woes. On 9 July he tears a calf muscle in a Twenty20 match. A few days later he is driving to the Surrey physiotherapist for treatment, when his car is hit from behind and he sustains whiplash. Five days later he tears a quad muscle 'lifting boxes' at his home. I determine to lift no boxes if I can possibly help it. 'Try lifting a finger instead,' says Polly, carrying in lunch.

Injury, though, makes you feel old. There's no other way of putting it. This is the way you can imagine feeling when you really are old and past it and waiting for the end. Suddenly you look in the mirror and see things you hadn't seen before. The tangled forest of nose hairs. Preternaturally long eyebrow hairs. And the inevitable ear shrubbery. They all seem to be trying to escape their natural habitats. Maybe they are trying to meet somewhere in the middle, for a party.

Your eyes look more watery than before, less focused. Your teeth look yellower, your gums look redder. Your smile, once thought charming, is now sinister. Your ears are beginning to grow. Soon they will be as large as Elton John's. One of the reasons men so often feel good about the way they look is that they don't look in the mirror that often. Their mental self-image is so much more reassuring than the real thing. But when you are feeling vulnerable, because your fucking foot hurts, you notice everything. Self-pity is even more unattractive than Elton John's ears.

You have to put these things into perspective. Earlier in the season, before we played Tusmore Park, I spoke to Chris Hart, the old friend who runs the team, and he said he obviously wouldn't be playing this year, what with the eye and everything. Eye and everything? It transpired that he had lost the eye the previous autumn in a horrific workshop accident, the details of which you really don't want to know. The other eye had only just been saved. And that was it: the end of cricket for him, for ever. He was being very chipper about it on the phone, as we probably all would be under the circumstances, being British. But what a terrible blow. Compared to this my injury was a mere scratch.

I continue to haunt Rain Men matches like a wraith. Actually I am rather enjoying not playing, and particularly enjoying not captaining. Tedious though it can be for regular captains to play and not captain, it's quite entertaining to stand on the sidelines and watch someone else deal with the stress, make all the decisions and take all the credit when we win. (Blast, blast, blast and damn.) The wickets are getting faster and flatter, too. (Bugger and bollocks.)

So for a while I have become a full-time spectator/scorer/umpire/irritant. Having played rather well during the annus horribilissimus when we lost nearly every game, I now watch as, without my taking part at all, the team start recording the occasional victory against reasonable sides. Our game against Somerton in July is typical. We have been playing them since we started, for their captain and fixture secretary is the aforementioned Gags, whom I have known since school, and who now lives in Somerton with his wife and children. The village side play three or four matches a season, and the rest of the time he comes and plays for us. When we were good we used to beat Somerton fairly easily;

when we became useless they started to beat us equally easily. They are our barometer opponents: how we do against them best reflects how we are doing generally. So this is a significant game. I clearly have to be there.

I'm not going to tell you exactly where Somerton play us. I will say that it's near the village and it's strikingly beautiful. All your most fevered fantasies of scenic cricket grounds are realised in this place, which is wondrously quiet and peaceful and has huge old trees in all the right places. You could argue that the pavilion is on the wrong side of the pitch to soak up the late-afternoon sun. Aesthetically, though, the pavilion is in exactly the right place, so I'd prefer to suggest that, in this instance, the sun is at fault. The wicket is a beauty. The teas are magnificent. There is one of those mobile scoreboard things you can sit in and pull all the levers. The bar is open all day. I have scored runs on this ground. If paradise has anything more to offer, I should be surprised.

Usually we are too busy playing cricket to enjoy the place to the full. (Perhaps if we come here when we die, we will have time then.) On this occasion, though, I have a full afternoon in which to loaf about. Polly and the kids have come along for the ride, as have several other families: there is more than enough room here for the children to run around and whoop it up and slip into neighbouring fields and menace sheep. My friends Stephen and Bella are also here. Stephen is one of my oldest and closest mates, who played for many years for Captain Scott despite being even worse than me. Once he scored a heroic 14 not out with a

crumpled Skol can down his pants in lieu of a box (which he
had left at home), but it gradually dawned on him that what
he really liked about cricket was (i) driving to matches at
high speed on his motorbike, and (ii) eating very large teas,
and that you didn't need to play cricket to do either. Having
reached 100 games, which seemed a milestone worth
achieving, he instantly retired, with some relief I think.
Bella, though, is Australian. Not only has she been raised in
a cricketing household, but she thinks Stephen should get
out more and do some exercise. The result is that both of
them have started playing for the team four or five times a
season. They come as a package, which I rather like. True, it
means we have two useless players instead of one. Neither of
them are what you might call mobile in the field. Indeed,
the Easter Island statues would be more fleet of foot. But
they are a good laugh and part of the gang. I only had room
for one of them in the team today, so they have decided to
share the place. One of them (Bella) will be doing the fielding and the batting, while Stephen will be concentrating his
energies on tea. They and the rest of us limber up with the
usual vast lunch in the pub round the corner.

I think this is the first time I have sat with the large
extended family grouping that sometimes congregates at
these matches. Gags's wife Caroline is there with a couple of
their children; several other players on both sides have
brought part or all of their broods along. Picnic blankets are
spread all over the place. Bulging piles of Saturday newspapers lie unread. Small children eat rice cakes and crisps and

drink mini-cartons of fruit juice. There seems to be no need to watch the cricket at all.

'Who's playing today?' asks one of the opposition wives.

Caroline goes through the list. 'And there's also Clive's brother-in-law from New Zealand, who everyone thought would be good just because he's from New Zealand, but he isn't, which is very funny.'

I eavesdrop on one of the children's conversations.

Child A: Which one's your dad?
Child B: The fat one, there.
Child A: What, that fat one?
Child B: No, not the bald one, the fat one.
Child A: The bald one's fat too.

And so on. One of the fielders drops a catch. His wife says, 'Oh God, he's going to be unbearable now.'

What if he scored 50 and took five wickets?

'Well, yes, he'd be unbearable then as well. But that would be a different sort of unbearable. A more . . . bearable sort of unbearable.'

A bowler takes a wicket. 'Oh look, Daddy's taken a wicket,' says his wife. She and her daughter exchange a glance, and laugh. Because I am limping, and not wearing whites, none of them see me as a cricketer any more. I have crossed the line. I am being allowed a glimpse into a side of village cricket I never knew existed.

Most cricket teams, as we have discussed, never bother

too much about the opposition. Even in the gentler climes of Rain Men, there are rivalries and niggles and contests between players, some more visible than others. When Terence fluffs a stumping, Howard at first slip will cry 'AWWW!!' as though the easiest chance in the world has been missed. A few years ago this was because Howard himself wanted to keep wicket, but then his back went and he had to acknowledge that his stumping days were over. (Howard never caught a thing behind the stumps, but would whip off the bails three or four times an over when he was feeling frisky.) But he still goes 'AWWW!!', even when the missed 'chance' wouldn't have been caught by a leopard. He says he does it to keep Terence on his toes. Maybe it's true. Maybe it's just a habit: he has done it so many times that it is now hard-wired into his brain. Or maybe it's a deep-seated resentment that Terence can still crouch down like that, even though he is five years older than Howard. These things hurt.

So, with all this going on, we pay little enough attention to the opposition, but we pay even less to our families, sitting fifty yards away on picnic blankets, unwrapping clingfilmed sandwiches. We have no idea what they are doing or saying. As a father you sometimes entertain fantasies that your children boast about you to other children: my dad's taller than your dad, my dad's richer than your dad, and so forth. As opposed to my dad's fatter than your dad, my dad's intrinsically more ridiculous than your dad. Close by, wives and girlfriends are enjoying a marginally more sophisticated version of the same conversation. My husband's sillier than your husband. Yes, your husband is sillier than my husband, but not by much.

This is, of course, treachery. But you can sort of see their point. There can be nothing more boring for them than to watch their husbands and boyfriends playing cricket for the afternoon and, worse, visibly enjoying every moment of it. They may be bitter, having long suspected that we like cricket more than we like them. But they must also be grateful, for, as a by-product of playing in such scenic surroundings, we have found somewhere for them to come and have fun too, while undertaking no tiresome childcare duties ourselves, as we are too busy playing cricket. In other words, we can have our cake and eat it. Then there's all the cake to eat. There is no downside to any of this. Consequently, our beloved partners can't quite formulate any killer arguments against our participation, but they have this vague feeling that we have got away with something, which of course we have. So we must pay for our presumption, and the currency here is respect.

Another problem may be the other wives and girlfriends. Cricket teams are only ever random collections of individuals who have been thrown together through love of the sport and the weird caprices of the individuals in charge. It therefore follows that the beloved partners of these individuals may not be the people your own partner ideally wants to spend an afternoon with. Or several afternoons every summer for several years. Other people's wives and girlfriends your wife or girlfriend can't stand are therefore your fault. She may even turn the whole situation around: here is a potentially glorious afternoon of rural relaxation and non-stop patisserie spoilt (as far as she is concerned) by the presence of Mrs Team-mate, who is a purse-mouthed sow with no conversation. These are the arguments that, as a couple, you would normally fall into at one in the morning when both of you have had too much to drink. But you must pay for it at other times as well, whether you are aware of it or not, and when you're out of earshot, letting through every other ball at mid-off, is as good a time as any.

Another reason for bringing the children is to try and get them interested in cricket. We all have dreams for our children. Personally I want mine to be happy and healthy and score Test centuries at Lord's. Neal has three daughters, and points out how much easier it is to play cricket for England if you happen to be female. His eldest daughter bowls in the nets from time to time, and she has it, whatever it is: instinctive length and line and a fair pace for a twelve-year-old. On his behalf we all dream of going to watch her take five-fors against Australia in around ten years' time, assuming that other things – such as what *she* wants to do with her life – don't get in the way.

So this season I have been bringing along my two-year-old son to a few games. When he asked for his own bat I paused for several seconds before rushing out to buy one. I haven't forced him to watch any of the Test matches on Channel 4: they were just on and he may conceivably have watched some or all of them. And I certainly haven't tried to coach him or engage his enthusiasm in any active way at all. I consider it wholly coincidental that he wants to play cricket at all times of day and night. Obviously it is my responsibility as a parent to play cricket with him whenever he wants to. Rather to my surprise he is a left-handed batsman, which makes sense, according to current orthodoxies, as he is right-handed in normal life. But I am right-handed both with pen and with bat, so he can't have been watching me much.

'Don't knock it,' says Howard. 'If he hasn't been watching you he clearly knows what he's doing.'

The extraordinary thing is that his technique is really quite impressive for a two-year-old. Straight bat, eye behind the ball, high elbow, good foot movement. Can you imagine how excited I am by this? You can.

'You're foaming at the mouth again,' says Polly.

We play in the front room, where the rug takes turn. We have a slightly weighted red tennis ball we found in a toyshop somewhere. 'Good shot,' he cries, after smashing the ball through mid-off. When he misses more than two consecutive balls he throws his bat away, lies down on the rug and cries. I don't tell him to get up. I feel like that most Mondays. He may as well learn now.

Since my injury, if anything, his enthusiasm has intensified. I may not be able to walk but I can still throw a weighted red tennis ball at him for forty-five minutes. He asks if we are going to the cricket on Sunday. I say we are.

He asks me if I'm playing. I say I'm not. Your bad foot, he says. Yes, I say. Is Robin playing? Yes. Is Simon playing? Yes. Is Howard playing? He smiles. These are his heroes now.

During our fielding innings my boy has had to run around with the other children, which he enjoys but regards as secondary to the main business of the afternoon. At teatime our fielders troop off, having restricted Somerton to . . . well, let's not bother with scores right now. All that matters is that they are thrilled with their performance, and can talk of little else.

'I love Battenberg,' says Robin. 'It's three cakes in one.'

When it's our turn to bat my boy unerringly seeks out the player who isn't in next and isn't scoring and hasn't anything much to do, and gets him to bowl at him. (If it weren't for the fact that he looks just like me, I'd swear he was Boycott's love-child.) Robin bowls at him for what seems like hours. 'Good shot!' I hear ringing out in infant tones. John who went to school with Kim Hughes also puts in the overs. Meanwhile, after the usual early collapse, Rain Men are heading towards a famous victory. Tim the formerly incredibly angry fast bowler is at the crease with Andrew-with-the-ponytail, whom we have forgiven after letting us down so grievously at Charlton a few weeks ago. Andrew, whose life I will later discover is in the process of falling apart, is in the form of his (falling-apart) life, having taken four good wickets earlier and now hitting a match-winning 36. There are several points to be made here.

- None of us knows that his life is falling apart, because no one has thought to ask him *why* he dropped out of the game at the last minute, and he probably wouldn't volunteer the information if we did.
- Having your life fall apart does not necessarily affect your form on the cricket field. Indeed, it could be that he is playing so well precisely because his life is falling apart.
- If we knew that his life was falling apart, which we don't, the rest of us would spend more time discussing whether having your life fall apart affects your form on the cricket field than discussing the fact that his life is falling apart, which doesn't seem any of our business.

Stephen is now in the nifty mobile scorebox, pulling the levers to update the score after every run scored. The winning boundary is hit and we celebrate with bottles of beer recently purchased, for Paradise has a bar that never closes. My daughter (five) approaches.

Martha: Are we doing well?
Stephen (glugging Becks): We've won!
Martha: We've won?
Stephen: Just now!
Martha: That's good. Because it's normally the other team that does that.

Great powers of observation, my girl. Either that or she's been talking to her mother.

19

BAD HABITS

From Ceefax, 16 February, 2003:

> Australian fast bowler Brett Lee feels his career can be prolonged by his decision to stop drinking beer.
>
> Lee gave up alcohol two years ago after suffering injury problems and a sore back which threatened his future.
>
> 'According to studies, athletes who drink alcohol are fifteen times more likely to get injured,' Lee explained.
>
> 'It does not matter whether you are having one beer or fifteen beers. I did not have a single drink for twelve months. It was not hard work, I felt very fit.'

We too feel very fit, especially after three beers at lunchtime. This page on Ceefax attracted my attention partly because of its bravery – in Australia, as I understand it, you just don't say things like that – and partly because I was surprised it wasn't made more of. Perhaps it was buried under other, less inflammatory news stories to protect our sensibilities. For cricket is awash with gargle. More even than rugby union, it is the drinking man's sport. At village level, we drink beforehand and we certainly drink afterwards, when we need it most. Against Somerton some people drank during the game as well. Like Everest, it was there. It would have seemed churlish not to. And yet most if not all of us would not dream of drinking at lunchtime during the week, when we are at work. We may have gone down the pub ten or fifteen years ago, when we were young and foolish and physically capable of processing the stuff. But now, as all wage slaves over forty must acknowledge, just looking at a glass of wine before sundown makes you fall immediately into a dark and dreamless sleep. Minutes or possibly hours later, you wake up at your desk having dribbled over your work and snored loudly. Everyone is laughing because, during your nap, you inadvertently named the female colleague you would most like to sleep with. In many companies you would be out of the building with your P45 and your black bin-liner before you could ask for a cup of tea.

Which itself may be one of the reasons you like a few drinks at the weekend. It is strange, though. When playing cricket, you would ideally be in possession of a clear mind and a body as tuned as a concert piano. Wilfully polluting both immediately beforehand seems like madness, and yet many of us do so every single week, with big daft grins splashed over our increasingly rubicund faces.

Anyway, hangovers are much more of a problem. A few years ago I played a game of cricket the day after my birthday party. This was a bad move. Not that I was capable of much movement. Thousands of miniature jackdaws were pecking relentlessly against the inside of my skull. In my stomach tidal waves of pure acid washed from side to side. I dropped three catches, two of them sitters. When I batted my fellow batsman was seeing the ball like a weather balloon, and was smacking fours all over the place. Whereas I was seeing it like a hydrogen atom, and was regularly crunched on the instep by nasty inswinging yorkers which, fortunately, I didn't feel. In the end I contributed yet another gritty 0 not out to a losing cause. I'll never drink again, I said to everyone after the match, eight seconds before tucking into a purely medicinal pint of something or other.

There seem to me a number of good reasons for having a drink or two before a cricket game.

1. It's fun.
2. It seems like a good idea at the time.
3. Why not?
4. If you're hungover it might actually do you some good.
5. It might take away some of your nerves when you go out to bat.
6. Particularly the nerves in your instep so you don't feel those nasty inswinging yorkers.

And drink is tolerated in cricket in a way that it tends not to be nowadays in many walks of life. It's part of the scenery. You sometimes hear people talk about the 'drug problem' in cricket, as though there was one. But, despite the fact that no one at all is strung out on hallucinogens or pumped up on steroids or even cursed with a snuffly nose twelve months of the year and liable to sudden mood swings, I have never heard anyone express the slightest concern that any cricketer might be, to use Sir Bobby Moore's deathless phrase, as pissed as a lemon. Buy a bottle of wine from the Co-op and you may spot the same warning on the label I once spotted, in between searching desperately for a corkscrew and almost tearing the cork out with my bare hands: 'Do not drink and drive, play sport or operate heavy machinery.' Play sport? I don't think I'd go out to bat at all if I didn't have a little something flowing through my veins. Although they may have a point about operating heavy machinery: drunken groundsmen running riot on heavy rollers are a menace to mankind.

And it's not just us lot: the real cricketers, as I see it, are just as bad. In Viv Richards's most recent autobiography – the one subtitled *The Definitive Autobiography* so we knew there wouldn't be another one out for at least a couple of years – the great man talked a lot about how scrupulous he had been throughout his career on matters of fitness and diet. Then, with rather more relish, he described the nights he spent carousing with I.T. Botham, whose unquenchable enthusiasm for good times has been well documented. The two of them appear to have consumed catastrophic quantities of gargle during the Somerset years, and the more they drank the better they seemed to play. How does Sir Viv square this? Well, to be fair, he doesn't, and being a genius he probably doesn't have to. If Lillee and Thomson can't knock you over, what chance have a few pints of scrumpy?

Australians, of course, are notorious. All fans of statistics know by heart the number of tinnies – fifty-four – consumed by David Boon on the flight from Sydney to London for the 1989 Ashes tour, which, let's not forget, the Australians won 4–0. Brett Lee must feel overwhelmed by the expectations generated by achievements such as this. Notice he says, 'It does not matter whether you are having one beer or fifteen beers.' What he means is, 'It does not matter whether you are having one beer or fifty-four beers, with another half-dozen in the cab on the way to the hotel.' Suppose you were an Australian fast bowler, indeed one of the fastest who has ever bowled, who operates within a macho environment in which several of your eminent forebears have grown enormous moustaches. And suppose that, by some freak of nature, you don't like beer. Maybe it makes you burp. Maybe you'd prefer a nice cup of tea. What do you do? You do what Brett has done, if you have any sense. Not that I am suggesting that Brett Lee would prefer a nice cup of tea to a foaming tankard of lager under any circumstances, because I do not wish to be sued for libel and go bankrupt and have to live on the streets drinking carpet cleaner. But I'm sure you get my drift.

As well as drinking, I find, cricketers also like smoking. Apparently, 27 per cent of the UK population likes a gasper, a figure that doesn't change much from year to year despite all the health warnings. A lot of those 27 per cent must play cricket. If you go into any dressing room immediately after the end of a match, be sure to take some air with you if you fancy breathing. The lighters all click on at the same moment, as though it's the slow song at a Tina Turner gig. Hear the lungs inhale in unison and relief, and wait for the first wracking cough of satisfaction. Not that everyone will be having their first cigarette since tea. Some will have been smoking right through the second innings. In Rain Men we have a simple rule: try not to smoke while batting, if you possibly can. But fielders puff away happily, and some of our umpires seem to live permanently in a small grey cloud of their own making. What sort of example are we giving to our children, who have to sit and watch all this? According to the children I have asked, a very bad example indeed. It's not big, they say, and it's not clever. (Next thing, they'll be sitting us down on the sofa and lecturing us on the danger of drugs.)

Again, real cricketers are equally at fault. I think instantly of Phil Tufnell, the smoker's smoker, who looked as though he should have been smoking between balls, and fielded with a spiritual butt between his lips. (In later years, stung by Australian taunts, Tuffers worked hard at his fielding, apparently by convincing himself that someone had hit a full pack of Rothmans down to long leg rather than the ball.) But there have been many, many others: Doug Walters, Shane Warne, John Crawley and now Robert Key, who owned up to smoking two fags during the tea interval when he scored his 221. It's odd, because no other sportsmen seem to smoke: at least, no other sportsmen who play sports that demand reasonable levels of fitness and athleticism. That leaves darts, snooker and golf – sports that, by remarkable coincidence, also involve a lot of drinking and are frequently played by fat men.

Why is cricket so tolerant of smoking and drinking? Maybe it's a certain strain of conservatism within the game, one that rejects wussy modern fretting about health issues and believes that what was good enough for Denis Compton is good enough for us. It may also be because chain-smokers and piss-artists are instinctively drawn to cricket as a game for chain-smokers and piss-artists: the 'virtuous circle' argument. There's also the simple fact that young people can abuse their bodies in these ways and, by and large, get away with it. Smoking, in particular, is a young man's game. Almost all non-cricketers I know have given up. They couldn't run up the stairs any more, and other feeble excuses. Of smoking Rain Men, though, only Neal has given up. And started smoking again. And given up. And started smoking again. Eighty-three times. He told me only last week whether or not he was smoking at the moment, but I have already forgotten. And he may well have started up again since, or given up, or both. Very confusing.

There's no doubt, though, that both smoking and drinking become more difficult as the years pile on. Like cricket, they both stretch the body to its limits. International cricketers retire relatively young these days, and some Test-level smokers I know have had to do otherwise. Drink is slightly more forgiving on the frame, in that it doesn't usually kill you in cold blood. Hangovers, though, are longer, and deeper: the dark mornings of the soul. And you are left with nothing to show for any of it, other than a beer belly. When you were very little you had a tummy; when you were young you had a stomach; now there's a belly down there. It rumbles and gurgles as though leading a separate life. You look down at it sometimes and think, where did that come from? It's nothing to do with me. And you think, if a belly could talk, what would it say? Probably something like: 'You'll have to field at first slip today, you fat bastard.'

Modern life has little time for bad habits. Smokers are constantly being hounded into ever smaller corners of the world where they are allowed to light up, and for drinkers the acceptable number of daily 'units' seems to fall every year, so that even moderate topers are made to feel like monstrous drunks. Cricket provides us all with a weekly bolthole. Other bad habits we can also indulge there include throwing tantrums, gross selfishness, trivial vengeance and cakes. You could see it as a form of therapy. To go out and behave atrociously from time to time is a fundamental human need, and probably keeps many of us sane. Cricket as universal panacea: it's an appealing idea. And if you can't play cricket for some reason, the next best thing is to watch it. It's not much good for your body, but it's excellent for your soul.

So off I go to Edgbaston, for a day of cricket with the chaps. (We don't think we have ever been lads, do not qualify as geezers, and have no wish to be guys. Our beloved wives and girlfriends think of us as 'the boys'.) What with one thing or another it has been a while since I have embarked on this kind of expedition. Indeed, the doctors said 'never again' but the promise of England vs Someone Else under floodlights, followed by a curry and a night in a sleazy businessmen's hotel, is impossible to resist. Some people travel all over the globe in search of thrills and excitement. We are going to Birmingham. Should we take the M1 or sidle artfully up the M40? The possibilities seem endless.

There's something peculiarly tragic about the sight of three middle-aged men let off the leash for the day. When I was fourteen and Harry and I bunked off school for the afternoon to see *Logan's Run* and *The Battle of Midway*, I could never have imagined that I would be experiencing the same visceral jolt of guilty pleasure the best part of thirty years later. History does not record the absolute bollocks that Chris, Nick and I talked in the car on the way up, which is probably just as well. Let it just be said that after checking in to the hotel, we go straight to the pub. Dutch courage, says Chris, for the main business of the day: smuggling alcohol into the ground. I won't tell you exactly how we do it, although I will say that my tapes of old *Mission Impossible* episodes come in very useful. Being able to go to the pub beforehand is one of the advantages of a day–night match, with the result that pole-vaulting directly into the R.E.S. Wyatt Stand with oxygen tanks full of Chilean Merlot holds few terrors. If that's what we do. Which obviously I'm not going to say.

Nonetheless, our restricted-view seats are a bargain at £35. We are almost behind the bowler's arm, in among a whole load of other men on naughty awaydays, and my view of the fat bloke's knees on my right isn't restricted at all. Over a full day's cricket you would hope to see these knees shift from bright Persil white through various shades of pink to a full ruby red, for, as British men of a certain age and weight will all agree, suncream is 'for poofs'. Sadly these knees are destined only to attain the colour of poached salmon. They have replaced the original occupant of the seat, who sat down, got comfortable, took off his shoes and poured his cup of tea, while staring dimly at his ticket, which was for seat 6 in the row, not seat 15. Fat bloke turned up, said, 'Oi! You're in my seat!' and the man moved with the gravest reluctance, as though he was doing the fat bloke a huge favour in allowing him to sit in his own seat. He then went and settled in seat 9.

The rest of the day, I'm afraid, passes in a bit of a haze.

James Anderson's first over goes for 19. Before the first ball the crowd cheer. Before the sixth they all laugh. This is the decisive characteristic of British audiences. We are the only people in the world who can mock and deride our own team *before the end of the first over.*

Chris goes to buy the beers, and gets stuck in a queue for forty minutes with four corpulent Yorkshiremen who are swaying dangerously. He has aged several years by the time he returns.

Various shouts from the crowd. 'Ooooh!' (whenever someone played and missed). 'YES!!!' (fielder 'caught' ball on first bounce). 'Hahahaha' (Anderson hit for another four).

After a batsman is out, a couple in row G stand up and snog. No one appears to notice.

The first innings comes to an end and the Tom Jones impersonator starts his act. It is my turn to buy the beers. In front of me in the queue (forty-five minutes) is a man who looks the spit of Thorpey, only shaved bald with the flag of St George painted over his head. So it may not be Thorpey after all.

As the shadows lengthen, the Mexican waves erupt. Blowers: 'The crowd is becoming rather noisy. I fear a Mexican wave may be coming on.' It has already completed three circuits of the ground and is starting its fourth.

The floodlights come on. As useful as a candle in a crypt, we think. Then, mid-evening, our eyes adjust and we wonder why every game isn't played this way. On a warm summer evening this is a wonderful place to be.

'I'd love to bat in front of a crowd like this.' That is the drink talking, unfortunately with my voice. Photos taken later that evening show a glassy-eyed pillock, not sure where or who he is. After a curry of quite staggering vileness, in a restaurant so empty it can only have been a front for organised crime, we stagger back to the hotel and I go to bed. Chris and Nick stay up and drink Jim Beam with representatives from the haulage trade. What a great day. I have some vague memory that England won, but I wouldn't be able to say for certain.

20

HIGH SUMMER, LOW SCORES

Off we drive to the badlands of rural Hertfordshire, and our first game against Chris's team, the Weekenders. As it happens, I have played against them once before, exactly twenty years ago with Captain Scott. We were all out for 9. For some reason we didn't play them again. Terence and I find the pub, sit in the back garden, next to a wasps' nest, move to the front garden, next to another wasps' nest, move indoors, check under the table for wasps' nests, sit down and order unfeasibly large meals. Sam the youth policy rushes in. He has just had another text message from Andrew-with-the-ponytail, who says he is suffering from food poisoning after a barbecue Sam knows he didn't go to. Twice in three games now, Andrew has dropped out at the last possible minute with desperately feeble excuses. (We still don't know that his life is falling apart: Sam won't let it slip for another couple of months.) Last time Andrew's name was mud; now it's shit. Why didn't he call two hours ago? Someone else did, on the off chance, to see whether we were a man short, and I had to say no. I call this person back. He is in Homebase with his wife and credit card. He won't be able to make it now. We are ten, and deprived once again of our opening bowler. We discuss possible punishments for the offending ponytail. They include:

- Two- or three-match ban, which wouldn't have any effect because he would have dropped out of those matches at the last minute anyway.
- Indefinite ban, accompanied by savage beating.
- Compulsory crewcut, administered by buzz saw.
- Car bomb.
- Slightly testy email, followed by complete forgiveness.

In the event we will quietly drop him from the rest of the season's games and send the slightly testy email. Meanwhile, we find our eleventh. A new player, friend of a friend, has brought along his girlfriend, and she volunteers. She hasn't ever played before, but she does have a very pretty hat.

We drive to the ground, following some detailed but opaque directions. We are a huge convoy of cars, taking wrong turn after wrong turn, driving in a big baggy semi-circle through a maze of country lanes, unaware that there is a short cut from the pub that takes two minutes. We know we have come to the right place because there is a man with red hair sleeping on a bench outside the pavilion. Roused by a team-mate, he disappears briefly inside, changes into the most creased clothes ever seen on a cricket pitch, trudges out and lies down in the outfield. Gloomy Bill, who is captaining today, wins the toss and elects to bat. I am crutch-free for the first time since my accident and elect to umpire.

Tim (umpiring at the other end): Want a guard, Neal?
Neal (abstractedly, like Sgt Wilson out of *Dad's Army*):
   Yes, that would be lovely.

Any resemblance between us and cobras waiting to strike remains purely coincidental.

The opening bowler roars in and bowls a few harmless ones outside off-stump. 'On the spot, Nick,' says a fielder. 'Come on, Nick, fire it up,' says another. 'Come on, Nicky boy, early wickets.' 'That's the knacker, Nicky boy.' (?) Next ball is way down the left-hander's legside. 'That's the length, Nicky.' 'Good ball to a right hander.' 'Got to want it.' 'Stay sharp.' 'On the spot.'

'They're all Australian,' says Neal. But only a couple of them are. They are the loudest ones, though.

'Bowling, Nasty Nick. Keep it up.' Neal plays a Chinese cut. 'Nasty!' exclaims the wicketkeeper with approbation. 'Keep it nasty, Nick,' says the captain. John, the other batsman, plays and misses. 'Great shape, Nasty!' Either these people have been coached, or they practise regularly. The bowling isn't bad, but the chirping is of the highest class.

We are a quiet side, by modern standards. Even our Australians are thoughtful and mild-mannered. And you can't force it. Chirping either comes naturally, or it doesn't come at all. The Weekenders have made the most of their talent. Some of their chirps border on the surreal. They also chirp as a team, sometimes building on the last man's chirp, sometimes swerving off on a wild chirp tangent. They remind me of the most amusing chirper I have heard in recent years, a teenage wicketkeeper who once turned out for the Warthogs. 'Bowl it on the money!' he yelled. 'At the wood.' Though normally possessed of an iron temperament, Howard spooned the next ball up to square leg. 'Hit the spot! Rearrange the furniture! Remember, Warthogs, hunger is the key!' Remember? Had they discussed this provocative notion beforehand? Sadly this boy was a lone chirper in a predominantly taciturn team, and we never saw him play for them again. I look around to see if he has joined this bunch.

Chris comes on to bowl. 'Fire it up, Duggo.' 'Good wheels on that, Chrissie.' 'Pitch it up, big boy.' (Hmm.) 'Bowling, Chrissy, that's perfect knacker.' 'Well bowled, the Islington Express.' (It's the definite article I like there. This is chirp that has been *considered*.) Nasty Nick is finding his line now. 'Pitch it up, Nicky boy. He doesn't like it up 'im.' Surely a contradiction in terms, I muse at square leg. The batsman is bowled next ball. He too has been undone by the paradox at the heart of this Mobius strip of a chirp.

The captain puts himself on to bowl. Bowls one ball, which is smashed for four. Complains of a pain in his shoulder. End of spell. *That's* the way to do it, I decide.

The wicket turns out to be a bit of a horror. As Chris will

later write in his match report, 'it was as dangerously unreliable as a Weekender's medical opinion, as inconsistent as his legal advice, as uneven as one of his BBC current affairs programmes and as bouncy as his breasts as he runs in to bowl.' The man who was asleep on the outfield earlier is thrown the ball and takes four for 5. We are all out for 94.

Bill (eating sandwich miserably): We should have bowled. Why do we always bat?

Me: Well, you're the captain.

Bill: But we always bat. It's team policy.

Me: Also, it's the temperature of molten lead out there. If we'd bowled, the pitch would have been flatter than a flat thing and they'd have scored 300.

Already it's turning into another of those games. If you think it sounds a little like *Groundhog Day* as you read it, think what it must be like to live it.

During their innings, which I can't bear to write about, I talk to Chris and his team and congratulate them on their chirp and their nicknames. One of their players, named Voulevitch, is nicknamed 'Va Va Voule'. Vickery is known as Morty. I am confused.

'As in "more tea, vicar-y",' says Chris. This is at least an improvement on adding the letter 'y' to surnames, as is the custom in the professional game. We may not do everything as well in village cricket, but on nicknames, at least, we have the edge. Steve James, the former Glamorgan and England opening batsman and now an astute writer on the game, tells a revealing story in his autobiography *Third Man to Fatty's Leg*. His team-mate Keith Newell was driving him and Mike Powell back from a team-bonding exercise:

> Keith Newell may be known for his rather laid-back nature but the rigours of an assault course on top of a sleepless night had left even the most resilient of us drained. So, as I rather selfishly dozed off in the back seat, I was suddenly awoken by Mike Powell in the front passenger seat, screaming 'Newelly!' There was a thud as we hit the central reservation of the A470 near Pontypridd. Newell had fallen asleep at the wheel but, thankfully, Powell had been resisting his slumber sufficiently to have noticed.

In other words, you think you are about to die, you just have time to scream one word, and that word is 'Newelly!' If you ever needed proof that professional cricketers are different to the rest of us, here it is.

Chris, though, is concerned at our lack of nicknames. Calling Terence 'the Human Sieve' is all very well, but Bill tends to be called 'Bill', Simon tends to be called 'Simon' and so on. We talk instead about injuries, of my ankle, of Francis's and Sam's broken fingers, of Richard's bruised hand, which still hasn't healed, and of Robin's brother, who played at Somerton and cracked a couple of ribs falling on the ball when he was supposed to be fielding it.

Chris: That must have been travelling a bit, to break a
    couple of ribs.

Me: Unless he'd got ribs made of biscuit.

Chris: Well, there's your nickname for him. Biscuit
    Ribs.

I realise I am in the presence of a master. We lose by nine
wickets.

Two weeks later we are playing the Railway Taverners in
north London. Simon and John have opened the batting.
This is by way of an experiment, forced upon us by holidays and injuries. Having scored some runs during the
season, Simon is more confident than he has been, but
that's still less confident than anyone else alive. At the crease
this translates itself into endless fidgeting, much chattering
and a strange refusal to call, because he is terrified of
making a mess of it. In a late-order batsman, somehow,
this is easily tolerated, but in an opening batsman, who
moreover has been scoring runs, it seems a little odd.
Simon, mesmerised by nerves, seems unable to overcome it.
John spent the entire winter in nets with Simon. He has
scored very few runs this season. And he can't bear chattering at the crease. This may not be an opening
partnership made in heaven.

Nevertheless they survive. Few runs are scored. In truth,
few balls are hit. Two batsmen are fighting their demons, and
not noticing that the wicket is flat and the boundaries are

short. Finally John tickles one through third man. He is unsighted, so looks at Simon, waiting for the call.

Time slows to a stop.

Simon is struck dumb. He is completely still.

There's at least one run here. There may be two.

John stares at Simon. His face registers pain, frustration, torment, murderous intent. Seriously, no cricket-playing jury would convict him.

Slowly, painfully, Simon's mouth opens. But, before a sound can emerge, the ball crosses the boundary. John can't believe it. He turns away from Simon and tries to calm down for the next ball. The umpires breathe again.

At the end of the over, Simon gestures to John to join him in the middle of the pitch.

John: What do you want?
Simon (attempting nonchalance): Just came for a chat.
John: The only words I want to hear from you are Yes,
    No and Wait.

'Of course, after that,' Simon explains later, 'I was too terrified to say anything.'

A long discussion in the pub afterwards about injuries. The Swedish tour looms and my ankle continues to throb. We wonder whether you are more inclined to get injured as you get older, or whether it just seems so because you take so much longer to recover. Although we sound like a load of old soldiers comparing their war wounds – 'It's only a bit of shrapnel' – the overwhelming mood is one of surprise that we haven't been injured more often. Being older, we all expected we would be spending most of our leisure hours on the treatment table, tending hamstrings, groin strains and the like. Not that any of us has a treatment table as such, but you know what I mean. What we had forgotten is that it's usually only fit people who suffer injuries. As John Emburey wisely observed, if you are going to pull muscles, you need to have some in the first place. Tim, in his days as the perennially angry fast bowler, was always exercising and keeping fit, and so crocking himself on an almost weekly basis. Whereas another player I could mention, whose gut is so large people are always asking him when it's due, never tweaked a thing.

In fact we have suffered no more than an average number of injuries over the years, and most of those were down to not getting out of the way fast enough, or, like my ankle injury, wholly unconnected to cricket. Some years ago we had a wicketkeeper, a lovely fellow, who played for us for a couple of seasons. Terrific stumper and useful middle-order batsman, he nonetheless suffered grievously from what used to be called the Johnny Giles but must now be renamed the Ashleys. One day he was in such discomfort that, fearing an unpleasant incident, he was compelled to insert one of his wife's Always Ultras in his jockstrap to stem the dismal flow. Tragically, while he was batting, this now sodden item somehow came loose, worked its way down his trousers and fell with a plop on to the pitch, marginally short of a good length. Soon afterwards he left the team, expressing the vague but heartfelt intention of becoming a Buddhist monk. Such are the effects of age. Or maybe not. He was only twenty-eight.

To Penzance for the weekend. On the train we all pretend to be receiving text messages from Andrew-with-the-ponytail.

'Apologies: unable to come this weekend,' reads Richard, 'Have been mauled by a leopard.'

'Kidnapped by aliens.'

'Appointed Chief Executive of the ECB.'

Simon has started playing for our friends the St Anne's All Stars as well as us, as one game a weekend no longer feeds his habit. He reports that on their website the All Stars are selling 'Yes! No! Wait!' t-shirts. And that one of the teams they play have started putting x-rays of their players' injuries on their website. We feel reassured that we are not alone.

Still, the weather is a worry. As last year we only have the one game on this 'tour'. If it is called off the hours will stretch out pointlessly until it is time to go back to London. Fortunately our hosts decide the game will go ahead unless the ground has been washed away by a tidal wave. It's still a toss-up. As Richard puts it, chances are that our opening batsmen won't walk out to the crease but row out there in small boats. Happily, the rain just about clears. In the event there will be just one brief stoppage during the innings, for Hurricane Ivan.

Simon goes out to bat with bootblack across his nose. He has seen Chanderpaul wearing what resemble small strips of tyre across his cheekbones during the summer's Tests, and has decided that this is what he needs to become the finished article as a batsman. He has scoured the internet and found this substance, which he has had sent over from America. The sun briefly emerges from behind the clouds and the bootblack starts to melt.

But who knows? Two years of non-stop coaching may have had little effect, but a few blobs of slimy stuff on the face seem to make all the difference. Simon scores 21, which includes an immaculately hit off-drive for four. Although he has yet to renounce his Trappist vows when calling, and still leaps away to square leg like a slightly portly gazelle whenever the ball is bowled short, he is at last beginning to look like the batsman he so wants to be. I won't be surprised if he scores a 50 in the next couple of years. It just shows you what's possible if you are clinically insane.

After that our innings rather subsides.

Terence: How were you out?

Stephen (stomping back): Caught by the wicketkeeper.

Terence: Was it an edge?

Richard (overhearing): No it was a cover drive, all the way to the boundary.

Eventually it is my turn to bat. This is my first match back. The ankle does not feel great. It is heavily strapped and

I am, in essence, unfit. But am I going to come all this way just to score and umpire and take notes for this book? I am not. So while a couple of our players go for a pee in the next field – there's no plumbing in the pavilion – I try and psyche myself into a batsman's mindset. I practise vicious pulls against imaginary long-hops. I play immaculate forward defensives that make my calf muscles squeak. I have a good look at the bowling, which is obviously completely harmless. A wicket falls.

I walk to the crease. I feel good. Even if I get out for 0 I won't be at the bottom of the averages. I have scored 6 runs so far this season but not been out. Several players have batting averages well below 6. I am safe. Deep breath. Robin Smith eye exercises. Take guard. Middle stump. Good, Terence is umpiring.

The bowler trots up. It's a high legside full toss. My eyes light up. The legside field is under-populated and it's all downhill to the boundary. I take an enormous heave and get a top-edge. The ball bobbles up abjectly to silly mid-off.

Oh God.

Oh shit.

That was probably it: my last chance to bat this season. The foot has been hurting all day and it isn't getting any better. I am going to Sweden whatever happens, but I suspect I won't be able to play what Bob Willis would call 'a full part'.

A wave of fury engulfs me. As I walk back to the pavilion, I berate Terence for not giving a no-ball. It was above waist height, but the bowler was very slow, so there is no way it could have been a no-ball. Trying to bully Terence in these circumstances is close to unforgivable. Getting out like that makes you think you look like a fool but you don't: anyone can get out like that. It's the way you react to getting out like that that makes you look a fool. I regret it almost instantaneously but it's too late. I pound back to the pavilion, which is strangely deserted. I presume everyone is trying to avoid me but I learn afterwards that a couple of them are now crapping in the neighbouring field, while several others have discovered that there will be mini-Jaffa Cakes for tea and have gone to stare at them. I sit alone and put my head in my hands.

Why oh why oh why oh why.

I breathe hard and deep. Slowly I can feel the anger and the humiliation beginning to recede. A few more minutes of solitude, and I shall be OK.

'Ahem.'

There is someone sitting next to me. Before I open my eyes I know who it is.

'How do you think I did out there?' says Simon. 'Should I have gone for the singles more? And was I still leaping away to square leg?'

According to witnesses, my eyes go black. My hands are shaking. I take a deep breath and prepare to speak.

21

SWEDEN

Sweden is not a traditional destination for cricket tours. Usually people prefer to go somewhere that is (a) warm and (b) full of people who play cricket. But England isn't particularly warm, except for the weekend when you don't have a fixture, and only a hard core seem to play cricket these days. The truth is, you can now find cricket being played pretty much anywhere on the planet. The hard core has gone global. Every country has one: it's just a matter of finding it and arranging a fixture with it. The Swedes found me, through a contact of a friend of a friend of a contact, and I was more than happy to be found. Slightly disappointingly, they don't translate all the more abstruse cricketing terms into their strange and musical language: for 'lbw' they say 'lbw'. They will say 'kasta bollen' for 'to bowl the ball' (but it actually means to throw the ball – there's no translation as such for 'bowling'). 'Spring!' means 'run!' but only as a verb; 'runs' are referred to as 'runs', because there is no noun for runs in Swedish. A batsman, happily, is a 'slagsman', which is exactly the way I feel as Terence and I drive into Stansted Airport in Essex at about four o'clock on a Friday morning.

Stansted Airport: what a bizarre place. As you stagger in, your eyes struggling to focus, your throat claggy with sleep unslept, you might expect it to be more or less deserted, save for the odd bomb-disposal squad blowing up someone's lost suitcase. But no: it's like Leicester Square at midnight on New Year's Eve. Where have all these people come from? Where are they all going? Wherever it is, it can't be costing them much. Only the prospect of a serious bargain would be enough to persuade this many people to forgo precious slumber in favour of savagely inconvenient travel. Already, the queues at Ryanair's check-in desks curl around each other, even though the desks don't open until five. Our flight is at 6.30. I stayed the night at Terence's, as he lives nearer Stansted than I do, and has the lumpiest spare bed I have ever encountered, which meant it was no great hardship to be roused from it at 3.30 in the morning. Nine of us are flying out today. The other two have gone out on the ferry. We have a full complement for this tour, or rather, we will have if everyone arrives safely at the other end. I am nervous, even though I am not in any sense in charge: Richard is match manager and has arranged the whole trip. But a 6.30 flight stretches the capabilities of the most dedicated cricketer. Will Robin make it? He is not an early-morning man. He is barely even a late-morning man. And what of Simon? So associated is he in our minds with random disaster that we cannot conceive that he will be there on time, even though he is getting a lift from his cousin, also called Simon. By 5.30 everyone bar the Simons has arrived, and bets are being taken.

I am a nervous flyer, who normally attempts to alleviate his anxiety with a swift drink or two beforehand, but there are limits. Which is to say that even I wouldn't think of knocking back several pints of strong lager in lieu of breakfast. On the other side of passport control, though, the bars are heaving. Huge burly blokes, whose dogs probably have tattoos, loiter menacingly in every strategic space. You dare not risk eye contact, in case they ask you ''Oo you lookin' at?' (I was once asked this by a bloke I wasn't looking at so I assumed he meant someone else. He then shouted 'OI!' so I looked up. He said it again ''Oo you lookin' at?' For half a second I thought about trying to explain the logical fallacy in his reasoning, before turning round and running away very fast indeed.) We sit at a table in the bar area, wussily sipping cups of tea. Other tea-sippers and croissant-nibblers come and go, but none of the drinkers ever seem to leave. Maybe they aren't flying anywhere. Maybe they are just getting royally pissed here twenty-four hours a day.

By five past six we are queueing at our gate. By Christ we look old. In your mid-forties, given a good night's rest and a hearty breakfast, you can just about pass muster as a human being by mid-morning. At 6.07 a.m., having consumed just four or five cups of airport tea, you can only hope you won't pass any mirrors. Cliff, who necessarily keeps bar-room hours, looks around seventy. The only time I have seen Robin look worse was when he broke his collarbone. I think about the hearty breakfast we shall enjoy on the plane – and then I remember we are flying Ryanair. As Terence points out, we will be lucky to get seats.

At 6.09 a.m. Richard returns from a recce to announce that the Simons have just shown up. Of our own Simon he reports that 'the light of derangement burns exceedingly brightly in his eyes'. I relax: we are quorate. 'Now all we have to worry about', says someone, 'is the plane falling out of the sky.' Everyone turns and stares. Oh God, it was me who said that.

It's another odd and random group of people, this cricket 'team' flying out to its doom. Simon's cousin Simon was the last to sign up, having been coerced by his relative on the reasonable grounds that we were absolutely desperate. Cousin Simon is a barrister and a hockey player aged thirty, although a magnificent rabbinical beard adds a few years. I am slightly jealous, having never been hairy enough to grow a beard like that, or a beard like anything much. It certainly adds to his authority when he goes out to bat. A few weeks ago he played for us in a village in Surrey to see what we were like, and also for us to see what he was like, for like so many people he hadn't played cricket since school. He turned out to be a natural sportsman, the sort of player who can score runs without trying, thanks to a good eye and what can only be some sort of instinct for correct technique. It's not just his beard I am jealous of.

There is, as ever, a hard core of regular tourists. Richard, Terence, Robin, Simon, Cliff and I would go anywhere at any time at almost any cost to play cricket, although all but Richard and Terence are perennially skint. The other two on the plane are Alan my neighbour (who is fifty-three and fitter than all of us) and Martin the former fast bowler (or former bowler, as Richard now classifies him). We all realise that this is a crucial weekend for Martin. His previous bowling spells this season have been so gruesome that a similar performance may compel him to give up altogether. Even last year he was only bowling seven- or eight-ball overs, and very rarely did the ball fail to leave his hand or land at his feet and roll abjectly along the ground to the batsman. (Or square leg.) He may just be rusty. A long net and judicious application of WD-40 may solve everything. As we take off I am nearly as preoccupied by this as by the possibility that the plane will explode in a gigantic fireball.

There are, thankfully, distractions. Richard reveals that when he is on a plane he waits to go the loo until he is flying over a country he doesn't like. Several times, he says proudly, he has shat on France. Meanwhile we study Ryanair's dual-purpose sickbag. You can chuck up into it, or you can send your films off in it to be developed. Or, if you're feeling surreal, both. Simon entertains us with his latest fascinating fact. Who were the first Allied civilians to land in Italy after the Second World War? Mr and Mrs George Formby. Robin, Cliff and one or two others drop into a deep sleep. I stare out of the window, just to make sure the wings are still stuck on.

We land at one of those little airports cheap airlines always use that are miles away from their advertised destination. As it happens this is good news for us as we are going in the other direction anyway, so are forty miles nearer where we are going than we would have been if we had landed in Stockholm proper. Also, I love small airports. No vast buildings designed by Sir Norman Foster, and no four-mile walk up and down stairs and along hundreds of identical corridors to collect your luggage which isn't there yet anyway. In a small airport, everywhere is a brief stagger from everywhere else, which is just as well, for as we queue at Customs Simon realises he has left his mobile phone on the plane. (In a few minutes he will discover that he has changed all his cash into the wrong currency.) Meanwhile I appear to have incurred a buttock strain while putting on my seatbelt for the final descent. It's an old injury which flares up from time to time, usually when Polly is there to mock. This time eight team-mates are there instead. Certain injuries never receive the respect they merit. The first time Terence ever kept wicket, he forgot to put a box in, and was soon writhing on the ground in the kind of agony only women in childbirth normally experience. And at least they get a sweet little baby at the end of it, whereas Terence's chances of fathering any sort of family seemed to be receding with every scream. My, how we laughed.

One bus- and one train-ride later we arrive, greasy and sweaty, in the small rural town where we are to play. Like all Sweden it is immaculately clean, as though a silent army of trolls creep in every night to hoover and buff it all up. How can they keep it so clean? By not making it dirty, I suppose. We, merely by our presence, seem to make it dirtier than it may have been in years. Our hotel, an old country house converted for the purpose, is particularly free of grime, as well as indecently pretty. The ground is a five-minute walk away. My buttock strain should be able to cope with that.

As we scoff up lunch in the hotel dining room, our last two players roll up in their motor. Stephen and Bella have, in effect, driven to Sweden. It has taken them a week, and it will take them another week to drive home. What for us is a sneaky weekend away is for them the centrepiece in a two-week driving holiday. Stephen loves driving. Fortunately, Bella loves Stephen, which makes it all possible. And they both love doing mad things like driving to Sweden with all the kit in the boot. For which we must all be truly thankful.

It is good to see them. I am fond of them both; and besides, I like having women in cricket teams. Even now, it can put the wind up more pompous oppositions, it still being the 1950s in some people's minds. We have had three women regulars or semi-regulars in our seven years. Unfortunately (for us, if not for them) Leona and Juliet have both had babies, which has temporarily removed them from even part-time cricketing activity. Leona's little boy must be three by now, so I am hoping to tempt her back soon. But for the time being Bella is the lone representative of her sex in our team. The first time she played, I was batting at the other end and, as usual, nervously looking for my first run. Bella hit her first ball to point and sprinted up the wicket without calling. Had a man done this, I would have stayed in my crease as though welded to it. But, as it was a woman, all my chivalrous instincts kicked in and I ran like a hare, straight to the bottom of the batting averages.

We hunt out our opposition, some of whom are staying in tents on the side of the pitch. This is true commitment. It turns out that only one of them actually lives in this town: the other ten have driven over from Stockholm. In supposedly non-cricketing countries you must be even more fanatical about the game to play it, although it may be that living in a non-cricketing country automatically makes you more fanatical. Guttsta WCC are run by an Englishman, Paul, and have a couple of canny Australians, but are predominantly Swedish. How weird it must be to discover this bizarre game from a foreign land and fall in love with it as utterly as these Swedes have. I think we immediately know that this weekend is going to be fun because these people are like us, except Scandinavian. Out of a slightly sloping field on the outskirts of a town like any other, they have created a cricket pitch, with an artificial wicket, a net in the far corner and a ramshackle pavilion full of foul-smelling old kit. They are delighted to see us as we are their first foreign visitors and even more delighted when we start practising and they see how useless we are. We, on the other hand, are experiencing that slight adjustment problem faced by all cricket tourists. You travel all this way, to a place more northerly than the Orkneys, somewhere unquestionably foreign and different and unfamiliar, and at the end of your journey you find a cricket pitch. It seems a miracle that it is there, and an outrageous stroke of good fortune. If there hadn't been a cricket pitch there, of course, we might have been a bit peeved. But discovering new cricket pitches in ever more unlikely locations never fails to give me a thrill. The landscape is unfamiliar, with darker and richer greens than we are used to, and snowy peaks looming on all sides. The Arctic Circle is just up the road. But some time tomorrow Martin will take the new ball and walk back to his mark and I will pray to a God I don't really believe in that he doesn't bowl a wide. Life rarely gets better than this.

The morning of the match. Simon proudly shows off his new injury. The previous evening he had had a net and been hit on the big toe. This is now so grossly swollen it looks like some sort of comedy prosthesis. We all express our deepest sympathy and run to fetch our cameras. Meanwhile, clouds gather, as if summoned especially. Paul, the Guttsta captain, says not to worry: the forecast is favourable and the pitch is artificial. So we settle down in the hotel grounds to a game of Kubb, which Simon has found in reception and been teaching everyone. It is a skittles game, rather addictive in fact. Soon, being hopelessly competitive, we are all surrounding the playing area (roughly the same dimensions as for pétanque) and cheering on one side or the other. Astoundingly, Simon turns out to be rather good at Kubb, even with an injured toe. In the event, he will remain undefeated throughout the weekend, which will swiftly erode everybody else's desire to play the game. For some people, I realise, not even the briefest moment of happiness or fulfilment goes unpunished.

After the usual massive lunch we waddle to the ground in our whites. We are looking forward to passing Swedes giving us funny looks, but there are none. At the ground Martin has arrived early and is tiring himself out in the nets. Paul proposes an unusual match format: two innings each, but each team's two innings add up to only thirty overs. You can declare your first innings closed any time between ten and twenty overs, and that determines how many overs you have for your second innings. I explain this to my team with care, as we enjoyed a late night out with our hosts last night and aren't feeling at our most intellectually acute. Shouldn't we save the rampant piss-artistry for our post-match celebrations? Of course we should, but it has never happened yet. The town only has one bar, which means we will be going back there again tonight. How sorry and sad is the British male, briefly liberated from domestic chains to rampage discreetly through the sleepy provinces of Sweden. Although after yesterday evening's indulgences, one or two of us are already talking dangerously about having an early night.

I win the toss and we move serenely to 1 for two off two overs. Terence goes first ball and Simon's cousin Simon stays around for two or three more. Richard and Alan my neighbour reconstruct the innings with care, when what we actually need is runs. When I declare on 60 for four after sixteen overs, it's with the feeling that we haven't quite got our tactics right. This is then confirmed, as the Swedes launch themselves at the bowling as though it's a Twenty20 match. The penny drops. It *is* a Twenty20 match. We're all enjoying the way each of them gets out for 7, giving Richard his best figures, five for 33, and Cliff four for 34. But the Swedes are scoring much more quickly, and wickets don't matter. Guttsta are all out for 92 in 18.3 overs. I mess with the order for the second innings, although not suffi-ciently to prevent Simon's cousin Simon from recording his second 0 of the match, this one a first-baller. We do not bat very well, it has to be said. The Swedes field like panthers, and both Australians can bowl. We manage 46 for five off our fourteen overs. This means they need 15 to win, and overs in which to do it. I open the bowling with the Human Sieve, whose donkey drops have been underused recently. The Swedes are without fear, or maybe they just don't care about averages. Terence takes two for 8 in his only over. Simon's cousin Simon comes on at the other end, despite never having bowled before in his life. He bowls a tidy maiden, during which Terence runs someone out. Now it's the turn of Robin, another lifelong non-bowler, mainly because he chucks the ball blatantly. He takes one for 7, his first ever wicket; Simon's cousin Simon comes back and takes *his* first ever wicket; and the Swedes scrape home on 16 for five, with 7.4 overs to spare and only their best players to come. How close can you get? Richard wins the Man of the Match award and the rest of the weekend passes in the customary haze. With the occasional amusing distraction:

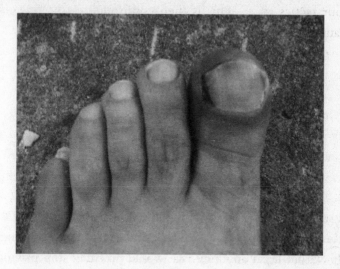

Why do we do it? Because if we didn't, someone else would, and if no one did, it would be an awful shame. And Martin? He did take a wicket, and his five overs only cost 21 runs, but this time he had two lengthy nets beforehand, and the wides still kept slipping out. I can feel him drifting away from us. Everyone has to retire at some point, we all agree the following day, over a beer in the airport. Except for me, each of us is thinking. I'll go on for ever.

22

INTIMATIONS

I suppose the big question is: what do we learn from any of this? And the obvious answer is: nothing, absolutely nothing. If we did learn anything, we would probably stop playing this absurd sport, which can only vex and disappoint and frustrate and send us to the brink of madness. Perhaps what we learn is that there is indeed nothing to learn, and if there is nothing to learn there is no point worrying about it. One of the stranger by-products of being in my mid-forties is that as well as becoming (like everybody else) much grumpier than I used to be, I also worry much less than I used to. Maybe intimations of mortality help you understand the supreme pointlessness of life. Or, if not understand, at least accept. Like smoking, drinking and football, wondering about the meaning of life may be a young man's game. We oldsters haven't got time to worry about this; nor, increasingly, have we the inclination. There's simply too much else to do. And there is less and less time left in which to do it.

Anyone who hasn't encountered death before the age of forty has been either very lucky or not paying attention. After your fortieth birthday, for some reason, people start popping off in droves, and you read the obituaries ever more closely. When I go on holiday for a couple of weeks I avoid all newspapers as a matter of policy, and miss them not at all. (I tend not to go on holiday during interesting Test series.) Whole political systems could have fallen and I wouldn't know a thing about it. But when I come back the first thing I want to know is: who famous has died? Have any significant comedians or wicketkeepers or newsreaders or backbench MPs met their maker? If Terence or Stephen didn't keep me up to date I might think that Irene Handl was still alive, among many others. (When Terence went abroad for six months I in turn sent him regular obituary clippings, which he had been missing even more than marmalade.)

And the best of all obituaries, needless to say, are in *Wisden*. In a *Wisden* obituary everyone's life is finally put into context. Many of us have spent years trying to do this, without notable success. Some people go into therapy. Others run into McDonalds with pump-action shotguns. Experience teaches us that the great questions of life, the universe and everything can never be satisfactorily answered, but a *Wisden* obituary probably comes closest. I was leafing through the 2002 edition only the other day. Sir Eric Edward Bullus, MP for Wembley North for many years, had died aged ninety-four. 'Although himself a virulently right-wing Tory, it is said he mourned the electoral defeat of Labour members with cricketing prowess.' We don't need to know any more; our imagination fills in the gaps. Then there was Richard Peter Hammond-Chambers-Borgnis, who had died in France aged ninety. 'Few can have enjoyed a sole first-class appearance of such dream-like quality.' He was a Royal Navy lieutenant and, as R.P. Borgnis, played for Combined Services against New Zealand in 1937. He came in to bat at 18 for four and scored 101 out of 180. He then opened the bowling and took three for 38. 'The New Zealanders won easily by nine wickets and that, as far as his first-class cricket was concerned, was that.' Of the rest of his long and no doubt distinguished life we learn nothing, except that he was distantly related to Sir H.D.G. Leveson-Gower, the lucky blighter.

Then I chanced upon John Perigoe Haynes, who had died in London aged seventy-four. He was a right-hand bat and medium-fast bowler 'whose solitary first-class match, at Fenner's in 1946, was a discomforting experience'. He was out for 0 twice and failed to take a wicket as Yorkshire stomped on the students in traditional northern fashion. 'John Haynes later taught at Cranfield Prep School and in New Zealand . . . and for 20 or more years was master-in-charge of cricket at Highgate School.' Which is where I went.

Blimey. 'Loony' Haynes.

I didn't even know he had died. And I certainly didn't know he had played first-class cricket. I had always thought of him purely as a geography teacher. Slightly shambolic demeanour. Leather patches on corduroy elbows. Faraway look, as though thinking of the Test match, which to his credit he usually was. Generations of boys had known of him only as 'Loony' Haynes, which seemed the height of wit in 1974. But he didn't seem to mind. After all, he had played first-class cricket. By my reckoning he had earned that faraway look. Maybe he was thinking, If only I'd turned that second ball to leg, I'd have got off the mark, and who knows what might have happened? Or maybe he was just pleased he had been given the opportunity to play at the highest level; he had been found out, and accepted it. As it is, his greatest cricketing achievement was almost certainly this obituary in *Wisden*. Too late for him to enjoy it corporeally, of course, but it makes a good case for the existence of an afterlife – always assuming there's a library there, with a full set of *Wisden*s on its shelves. (A reasonable assumption to make, I would say.)

So 'Loony' Haynes got what we all want – an obituary in *Wisden* when we die. As final judgements go, it beats St Peter into a cocked hat. Incidentally, if there's such a thing as reincarnation, I'd like to come back as someone who can time an on-drive.

Does seventy-four seem a reasonable age to go? Probably, unless you're 75 not out.

In June 2003 an old friend of all of us, Cie Malde, was batting for the Railway Taverners on one of several pitches artfully hidden in the valley between Muswell Hill and

Crouch End in north London. By all accounts he was playing as fluently as ever, and at 75 not out he pulled a short ball for four – one bounce and over the boundary. But before it bounced, Cie (pronounced as the letter 'C') collapsed in a heap. He had suffered a heart attack. He probably never knew a thing about it. He was fifty. Well, that's what he had told everybody. According to the local paper he was fifty-one. At his funeral his brother told me he was forty-nine. For years Cie had been adding years on. But it was characteristic of him that he would want to reach his half-century as quickly as possible.

A huge number of cricketing people in north London mourned his passing. Apt as we are to get sentimental, it's customary to say what a fantastic bloke the deceased was, whether he was or not. But Cie genuinely was a fantastic bloke, as sweet and kind a man as you could hope to meet. Utterly unselfconscious, without any side to him at all, he must have made thousands of friends in cricket. Hundreds were at the funeral. I have never seen so many cricketers cry. His large extended family were touched by the affection he had inspired, but not, I think, greatly surprised.

For Cie was the most cricket-mad person I have ever known. I have written here of Simon, whose newly minted obsession seems likely to lead to some form of residential care. But Cie lived the life for twenty years. He was introduced to the game at the age of thirty by Mick Jagger's brother Chris, and ended up playing four or five games a week every week every summer for more clubs than anyone knows about. This is a man who started a nightclub because it would free up his days to play cricket. The Taverners first encountered him in the mid-1980s as one of the few sociable members of an opposition side renowned for their cussedness. Cie jumped ship and ended up playing 255 games for the Taverners, as well as 135 for the Magpies and 121 for Captain Scott, where I first met him. As well as opening the batting, Cie bowled delightfully loopy and canny off-spin, with a well-disguised change of pace. Most teams used him as a batsman who could bowl, but for Scotts, always short of bowling, he was a bowler who could bat. If the pitch wasn't helping him, Cie would nip off between overs to smoke an enormous joint in neighbouring woodland, and emerge minutes later as twice the bowler and, sadly, half the batsman. Not that he seemed to care much, as he played for the pleasure of it rather than the figures, and enjoyed his team-mates' successes as much as his own. Again, you often hear this said of people; this time it's true.

His funeral was curiously enjoyable. We all drank a lot and exchanged stories. The time Cie ran on to the field at Lord's to congratulate his hero Robin Smith on a century, only to find that he was being chased and apprehended by his team-mates from the Taverners, who were working as stewards for the day. His determination, when we went on to tour to Rome, to go and meet the Pope. His incomprehension at the Pope's determination not to meet him. Dancing with Desmond Tutu on the pitch at Newlands in 1996. Trying to chat up Robin's girlfriend in a pub in Crouch End with the line 'I've played cricket with Hugh Grant.' Nicking a single off the last ball of an over, then laughing infectiously if anyone suggested that he had done it on purpose.

Wandering home with a big boozy smile on my face, I reflected on how lucky we are to be cricketers. Football is now a vast multinational business, its grandmother long since sold to the highest bidder. Cricket, though, is just a big club – the only club, really, you would want to be a member of. When one of the Taverners said wistfully, 'He was only 25 runs away from a century,' we all went quiet. We knew exactly what he meant. Then someone said, '21 runs away. He must have known it was four as soon as it left the bat.' We went silent again. Fancy thinking that as your last thought on earth.

It has to be the only way to go. Hasn't it?

POSTSCRIPT

March 2005. Martha (aged five) is practising her writing, while James (aged two) scribbles away on his own sheet of paper, just to join in. I am supervising (i.e. reading paper).

Martha: Daddy, how do you spell 'children'?

I tell her.

James: Daddy, how do you spell 'Shaun Pollock'?

That's my boy.

POSTSCRIPT FOR THE PAPERBACK EDITION

In April 2005, as the hardback edition of this book was being printed, Tim the fast bowler rang up.

'Bad news. Harry has lung cancer.'

I was astounded and appalled. Harry had never smoked a cigarette in his life. In 1975, when we were both fifteen, the two of us had organised a semi-official school trip to Bath and Bristol and cleared an impressive (and unofficial) profit of £20, which we spent on an afternoon of merriment in Leicester Square, seeing *Logan's Run* and *The Battle Of Midway* back to back. That same day, in an excess of high spirits, we bet each other £20 that the other one would be the first to start smoking. Such was the intensity of our rivalry that, as a consequence, neither of us ever did smoke. In the intervening years we congratulated each other regularly over our good fortune. So why did he get lung cancer? It still seems monstrously, viciously unfair. Harry was determined to beat it. When we were at university his mother was diagnosed with breast cancer and given six months. She lived for another ten years. With blithe disregard for the survival statistics (which gave him little chance), all Harry's friends took it for granted that he too would go on indefinitely. If anyone could overcome the odds, we agreed, he could. Indeed, almost the most upsetting aspect of all this was the immediate surrender of his 100 per cent appearance record for Captain Scott. The team had played 640 games at this point and Harry had played every one. He actually started to play the 641st. Sean Reilly, a good man and powerful opening bat who will now run Captain Scott, was late back from holiday, so Harry went out to bat in his absence, although he could barely stand up. When Sean arrived he told him to get off the pitch. Harry agreed and so, like Cie, remained not out in his final innings. He wrote in the scorebook 'Retired due to cancer'.

Harry died on 7 November 2005. I had known him for thirty-five years, and had been banking on another thirty-five. He leaves a wife, Lisa, two children from his first marriage, Betty and Bill, and many, many stories of his exploits. This paperback edition is dedicated to his memory.

January 2006

ACKNOWLEDGEMENTS

My thanks to Richard Beswick of Time Warner for his encouragement, editorial nous and, of course, money; to Iain Hunt and Kirsteen Astor for making the process painless; to my agent Patrick Walsh for oiling the wheels; to the regulars and occasionals in Rain Men CC, notably Cliff Allen, Stephen Arkell (who came up with the title), Simon Canter, Ross Clark, Leona Cobham, Ruairi Conaghan, Tim Cooper, Richard Corden, Sam Craft, Alan Doggett-Jones, Martin Dyckhoff, Bella Goyarts, Conrad Hall, John Haydon, John Hondros, David Jaques, Andy Leonard, Andrew Mackay, Leo McKinstry, Howard McMinn, Bill Matthews, Stephen Mills, Francis Peckham, Neal Ransome, Simon Rose, Terence 'Human Sieve' Russoff, Jeremy 'Biscuit Ribs' Welch, Robin Welch (who found the cover photo), Juliet Wheaton, Alan White, Charlie 'Dinnerparty' Williams and Tim Young; to fellow sufferers Maxie Allen, Binky Beaumont, Christopher Douglas, Paul Eade, Paul Finck,

ACKNOWLEDGEMENTS

Tristan Haddow-Allen, Chris Hart, Eileen Heinink, Tom Holland, Richard Howard, Steven Lynch, Nick Newman, Mike Payne, Sir Tim Rice and Andy Robson; to Ian Hislop, Simon O'Hagan, Chris Pollikett, Kate Saunders, Mitchell Symons and Russell Taylor for their friendship and advice; to Tim de Lisle, Stephen Fay and John Stern for commissioning some of these jokes in the first place; to Harry Thompson for his help and generosity; and to Paula, Martha and James for everything.